THE HARPER COLLINS
BUSINESS GUIDE TO MOSCOW

THE COMPLETE GUIDE FOR THE BUSINESS TRAVELER

THE AUTHORS

EUGENE THEROUX, a Washington-based attorney with extensive experience in the Soviet Union, is partner in the law firm of Baker & McKenzie.

FREDRIC M. KAPLAN, co-author of the best-selling *China Guidebook,* has traveled the length and breadth of the Soviet Union.

ERIC SEMLER was a visiting journalist at the Soviet newspaper, *Moscow News,* and is co-author of *The Language of Nuclear War.*

HELEN SPERANSKY recently emigrated to the U.S. from the U.S.S.R., where she worked extensively in international travel and trade sectors.

THE HARPER COLLINS
BUSINESS GUIDE TO MOSCOW

Eugene Theroux / Fredric M. Kaplan
Eric Semler / Helen Speransky

PERENNIAL LIBRARY

HARPER & ROW, PUBLISHERS, INC.
New York

EURASIA PRESS
Teaneck, New Jersey

Produced by Eurasia Press,
168 State Street, Teaneck, NJ 07666-3516

ISBN 0-06-096853-2

90 91 92 93 94 10 9 8 7 6 5 4 3 2 1

CONTENTS

VI   JOINT VENTURES / 107

VII   SOVIET LAWS / 123

VIII   U.S. EXPORT CONTROL REGULATIONS / 127

IX   RUSSIAN LANGUAGE GUIDE / 131

X   APPENDIX / 151

PREFACE

This is a guide to a city at the center of sweeping political and economic reforms that are dramatically changing the Soviet Union and the face of the world. No one can predict the outcome, any more than anyone could have predicted that the Communist Party's Central Committee would vote to relinquish its monopoly on power and permit opposition groups to compete for the right to govern.

Amid the changes, uncertainties and expectations abound. While it is difficult to know what kind of regime will eventually come to rule the Soviet Union and its former satellites in Eastern Europe, political and economic forces have led the Communist Bloc to seek help from the West in the form of loans, technology, joint ventures and more open trade.

Western companies appear eager to explore the new opportunities in the Soviet capital. We hope this book will guide you to the doorstep of this new era, and provide information that will help you in your business dealings and visits to Moscow.

The Authors

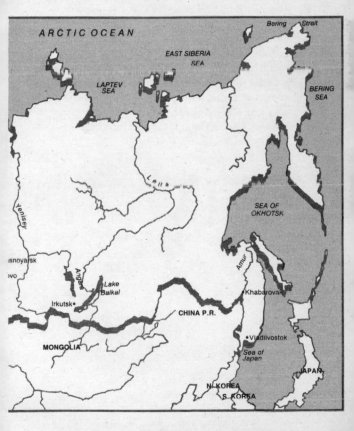

ACKNOWLEDGEMENTS

The illustrations that appear throughout the book were drawn by Eugene Theroux, and are gratefully acknowledged. The authors also wish to acknowledge, with thanks, Dr. John P. Hardt for the historical chronology appearing in the Appendix. Eugene Theroux thanks Naomi Kennedy, his secretary. At Eurasia Press, the skills and dedication of Eileen O'Connor, Managing Editor, and Patricia M. Godfrey, Senior Editor, are deeply appreciated. Special thanks to Marci Barris, the book's designer, and to Alan Barris, Chris Yarusi and Karen Bailey of Logic Communications, Inc. for their perseverance and skill. Anat Kaluzshner prepared the excellent maps that appear throughout the guide. At Harper & Row, Carol Cohen and Mary Kay Linge were supportive from the start, and deserve much credit for the fruition of this project.

THE U.S.S.R.
IN BRIEF

WELCOME TO MOSCOW

More than 8.5 million people live in Moscow, a strange
but fascinating metropolis that lacks the efficiency,
comforts and conveniences that are commonplace in
nearly every other world capital. Even the most well-
informed tourists are taken aback by the city's comparative backwardness. In many shops and restaurants,
prices are totaled on abacuses, not machines. Common
amenities taken for granted in the West, like taxi cabs,
restaurants, mail or travel by air, often involve hassles
and disappointments for the business visitor. A striking
exception is Moscow's spotless and museum-like *metro*
system, where, during rush hours, the average train
arrives every 50 seconds (just to be sure, clocks above the
platform count the time between trains).

The city of Moscow is arranged within concentric
rings, with the Kremlin at the very center. The city lies
in the central zone of the great Russian Plain on the
banks of the Moskva River, about 360 feet above sea level.
Moscow's history spans about 2,000 years, although it
was first mentioned in annals in 1147 AD when Prince
Yuri Dolgoruky (Yuri the Long-armed) founded it as a
wooden fort, or *kremlin*. In the 13th and 14th centuries,

Mongolian Tatars invaded and ruled Moscow. By the 15th century, Russian princes had regained control and built Moscow into a strong and prosperous capital of a unified Russian state. It remained the economic and cultural center of Russia, even after Peter the Great decided to make St. Petersburg (now Leningrad) the capital in the early 18th century. Vladimir Ilich Lenin, the architect of Soviet Communism, returned the capital to Moscow in the spring of 1918, several months after he had led the Bolshevik, or October, Revolution in 1917.

Today Moscow is more than the center of the Soviet government and power. It stands, as always, the embodiment of the Russian character and history. On a stroll down the capital's busy downtown streets, you will encounter many contrasts. Most of the Soviet Union's 100 different ethnic groups are represented in Moscow's population. You will feel the pulse of a vibrant city, but will also detect remnants of a history and culture brought to a halt in 1917. Long rows of government buildings alert you to a colossal bureaucracy at work. At the same time, colorfully ornate Baroque structures, like the Bolshoi Theater, the buildings inside the Kremlin, and beautiful onion-domed churches, remind you of a Russia ruled by powerful czars and wealthy nobles, and one in which religion was very important.

A trip to Moscow is more of a challenging adventure than a relaxing vacation. The adventure these days is more enjoyable and interesting now that political and economic reforms by the Soviet government have led to an increase in private enterprise and diversity within Moscow itself. New, privately run cooperative restaurants, grocery stores, travel agencies and medical clinics offer higher quality goods and services (at higher prices, of course). In addition, there is a greater willingness on the part of English-speaking Muscovites to engage foreigners in conversation.

Despite the recent changes, Soviet citizens endure hardships unknown in any other industrialized country. They wait longer than ever in lines for such basic products as milk, fish, meat and vegetables. These foods, as well as sugar, flour, cooking oil and fruit, are scarce and expensive. Meanwhile, growing numbers of black marketeers (known in Russian slang as *fartsovschiks*) besiege tourists with offers to trade Soviet rubles and souvenirs for Western clothing and currency (at the time of this writing, one dollar was worth 15 to 20 rubles on the black market, while the official tourist exchange rate was about one dollar to 6 rubles). Incidentally, law-abiding visitors need not despair. It is possible to legally and cheaply buy many of the popular Soviet souvenirs, such as *matroshka* dolls, fur hats, military watches and lacquer boxes at the extremely popular outdoor flea market in Moscow's Ismailavo Park, or in more expensive foreign currency stores, known as *beryozkas* (Russian for "birch tree"), that are located in most hotels and scattered throughout the city.

To Westerners, Muscovites are unusually warm and forthcoming, but with one another they are often churlish. A ride on the subway or bus during rush hours can be bruising, and don't expect to hear an "excuse me" (*izvenitya*) from a Russian who accidentally jabs you with an elbow on a crowded bus or train. That same Russian may later eagerly seek your friendship and insist that you have dinner in his state-owned apartment, where the simplest yet most delicious Russian food is likely to be prepared.

GLASNOST, PERESTROIKA AND GORBACHEV

Winston Churchill once described the Soviet Union as a "riddle wrapped in a mystery inside an enigma." Even as the Soviet Government and its people exhibit new openness in the midst of a severe political and economic crisis, the world's largest country remains an enigma, surrounded by questions: In what direction is the U.S.S.R. headed? Can it surmount ethnic and linguistic separatism and economic and political stress? Can it actually turn itself around? If so, how? Who will lead the change? What type of foreign support will the Soviets receive? And what will the country be like in a few years?

No one, not even the Soviet leadership, seems to know the answer to these questions. The events of 1989 and 1990 — the sudden collapse of Communist regimes in Poland, Hungary, Czechoslovakia, East Germany, Bulgaria, Romania and Mongolia, and the drive for secession by several Soviet republics — indicate that Soviet-style communism is highly vulnerable and lacking in broad, popular support. But the strong, centralized Soviet government led by President Mikhail Gorbachev has showed no signs of withering away.

Glasnost and Perestroika. It was Gorbachev's leadership and unwillingness to block democracy movements in Eastern Europe that triggered the dizzying changes in the Soviet Union and abroad. Gorbachev has sought to transform his country economically and politically, using two words that have entered the global vocabulary — *glasnost* ("openness") and *perestroika* ("restructuring"). He first used these terms in a December 1984 speech, three months before he became General Secretary of the Communist Party. In the spirit of these two words, Gorbachev began a reform of the Soviet State and the Communist Party. He has released scores of Soviet dissidents, allowed Jews and other minorities to emigrate, unilaterally reduced troops and conventional weapons, agreed to cut the Soviet nuclear arsenal, tolerated anti-Soviet publications, permitted the country's first free elections since the Revolution, ordered the rewriting of Soviet history books to expose the truth of an ignominious past, and helped bring the Cold War toward an end.

Kremlinologists say that more than anything else, Gorbachev's program is motivated by a need to reform the rapidly deteriorating Soviet economy before it collapses altogether. For years, it has been plagued by a monstrously inefficient bureaucracy, huge deficits, a currency that has no value on the world market, declining industrial and agricultural productivity, worker indifference, widespread alcoholism and alarming shortages of consumer goods and housing.

Despite grumblings from party bosses reluctant to release their tight grip on the faltering economy, Gorbachev has shown an interest in Western, capitalist models and has promoted selective free-market principles. In an effort to attract foreign currency, he has encouraged and invited Western companies to engage in joint ventures with Soviet firms. Gorbachev has also allowed Soviets to run their own cooperative firms and restaurants. Thus far, however, the Gorbachev reforms have yet to succeed in reversing the economic slide.

An Insider's View. If you talk to Muscovites, many will tell you their lives have never been worse. Stores are virtually empty, prices are soaring and the black market is thriving. In Moscow, a shortage of vacant apartments forces most young married couples to live with their parents and forgo having more than one child. Such modern conveniences as microwave ovens, dishwashers and washers and dryers are rarely found. Recently, an American diplomat beginning an assignment in Moscow after a two-year post in Mexico City quipped that the Soviet Union makes Mexico look like a superpower. Another characterized the U.S.S.R. as "Burkina Faso with nuclear weapons." On the other hand, it is possible to find almost anything you want in the Soviet Union — as long as you know the right people or belong to an elite layer of society. Corruption is rampant, fueled by a growing Soviet "mafia" and seasoned black marketeers.

Many Soviet citizens regard Gorbachev as a superficial chatterbox who pays too much attention to foreign affairs and not enough to domestic problems. They view him as a power-hungry international superfigure, a party man not to be trusted, who has ignored the economic needs of the Soviet population in his effort to make the world a more peaceful place. Many people desire speedier material and political change, and are aligning themselves with rival groups outside the government. These days, political rallies are commonplace in Moscow, although it is often unclear who is rallying and for what purpose.

Gorbachev's opposition is fragmented. One faction is led by the maverick Boris Yeltsin, a former member of the Politburo and a vociferous critic of Gorbachev. But he lacks broad appeal. Popularity is growing for Russian nationalists, who oppose both communism and Western influence. They advocate a state rooted in Russian values, one with a non-capitalist economy and a universal Russian language. Disturbingly, they are allied with — or at least not disaffiliated from — the burgeoning anti-Semitic organization known as Pamyat ("Memory") and other xenophobic groups.

An Outsider's View. A visit to Moscow leads many tourists to ask whether the Soviet Union's backwardness is the fault of the communist system, or of the Soviet people themselves. The answer may be that both are to blame. The inefficiency of the system causes low morale, and Soviet citizens seem to take every opportunity to complain about their lives, jobs, government and fellow countrymen. Many may annoy and depress you with their repeated requests for help in leaving the country. Employees in restaurants and shops may shock you with their blatant dishonesty. Often, they lie because they are too lazy to make an extra effort.

In the last few years, Soviet curiosity about the West has soared. Americans and West Europeans are envied for their freedom, prosperity and opportunity. To Soviets, foreigners are walking Christmas stockings. They covet American products; some will not hesitate to make you an offer for the shoes on your feet or the money in your wallet. Just a few years ago, Soviets with relatives or friends in the U.S. were suspect. Today, an American connection is a status symbol.

After spending some time in Moscow and observing the inefficiencies and shortcomings of Soviet life, you may wonder how the West ever came to fear the U.S.S.R. After all, this is a country where nearly everyone — from common citizens to wealthy tourists — must beg for service, worry about the next meal, wait hours or days for a telephone connection, wait in line for hours for inferior food products and ride on airplane seats with missing seat belts. Conversely, the Soviet Union occupies a leading role in space exploration; commands an enormous nuclear arsenal; and maintains a huge, well-disciplined military. With all of its problems, the U.S.S.R. is still the world's largest producer of wheat, butter, iron ore, steel, books and cigars, among many other commodities.

The big question on many minds is whether Gorbachev can survive the great changes and events that he himself has set in motion. Even the Bush Administration has had trouble deciding how far to extend its hand to the Soviet President. Some American Democratic leaders have urged the Bush Administration to provide direct economic aid to the Soviet Union to reinforce Gorbachev against challenges to his power. In a world where power is now measured more by economic strength than military might, the Soviet Union's very survival will be at stake as it struggles to improve the conditions of its own people and compete as a world economic power.

THE SOVIET GOVERNMENT

With Mikhail Gorbachev's *glasnost* and *perestroika* in full swing, important and far-reaching changes are occurring in the structure of the Soviet government. At present, Gorbachev occupies the recently created and significantly empowered post of Executive President of the country, having been elected by the Congress of People's Deputies in March 1990.

Gorbachev has appointed a presidential cabinet that will function as a senior advisory and policy-making body. This group is likely to replace the Communist Party's Politburo in terms of function and power wielded. The council consists of: Alexander Yakovlev, foreign policy expert; Eduard Shevardnadze, Foreign Minister; Dmitri Yazov, Defense Minister; Vladimir Kryuchkov, KGB Chief; Nikolai Ryzhkov, Prime Minister; Yuri Maslyukov, First Deputy Prime Minister; Albert Kauls, legislator; Chengiz Aitmatov, novelist; Stanislav Shatalin, academic; Vadim Bakatin, Minister of the Interior; Valeri Boldin, Central Committee, CPSU; Yuri Osipian, academic; Veniamen Yarin, legislator; and Valentin Rasputin, novelist.

The Congress of People's Deputies consists of approximately 2,250 members, of whom 1,000 are chosen by various organizations and 1,500 are directly elected by the people. The Congress functions as a parliament, and its debates are often televised in the Soviet Union.

Between sessions of the Congress of People's Deputies, the legislative business of government is carried on by the Supreme Soviet. This body, selected by the Congress of People's Deputies, consists of 542 members and stays in session for about eight months of the year.

The Executive President is advised by a Council of Ministers, whom he appoints, consisting of 86 members. This body usually meets four times a year.

There are 15 Republics in the U.S.S.R., the largest of which is the Russian Republic.

THE COMMUNIST PARTY

Until 1990, the Communist Party enjoyed constitutional assurance of a monopoly on political power in the Soviet Union. That has changed as the U.S.S.R. has moved toward a multi-party state. Policies of the Communist Party of the Soviet Union (CPSU) are determined by Party Congresses that are held about every five years. A Party Congress scheduled for the summer of 1990 will address major party reforms recommended by the Central Committee of the CPSU, which met in February 1990. With broad powers now vested in the office of the Executive President of the Soviet Union, there is no guarantee that Party policies will automatically take effect, as in the past, as national policies.

The Central Committee consists of 357 members, 249 of whom are voting members chosen by the General Secretary of the Party. Mikhail Gorbachev presently serves as General Secretary of the Party as well as Executive President of the U.S.S.R. The Central Committee selects a Politburo of 11 members that meets regularly to oversee national policy. As the post of Executive President evolves, it is expected that the primacy of the Party and its governing apparatus, the General Secretary, the Politburo, the Central Committee and the Party Congress will diminish.

PEOPLE AND LANGUAGE

With a population of 287 million, the Soviet Union is the third most populous country in the world, after China and India. Most Soviets reside in the European part of the country. Vast reaches of the north, central and eastern sectors of the country are very sparsely populated.

Ethnic Russians constitute about half the total population. Taking the Russian, Ukrainian and Byelorussian people together, the Slavic population of the Soviet Union is about 215 million, or about 75% of the total. The remaining population of about 60 million is composed of some 120 nationalities speaking about 50 languages. The Russian language predominates in the U.S.S.R., and is the first language of about 60% of the population. Moscow, the capital and the U.S.S.R.'s largest city, has a population of about 8.5 million. The next largest city, Leningrad, has about 4.8 million people, followed by Kiev with about 2.4 million.

GEOGRAPHY AND CLIMATE

In land area, the Soviet Union is the largest country in the world. Spanning 11 of the world's 24 time zones between the Baltic and Bering Seas, the U.S.S.R. covers 8.6 million square miles, about 22.4 million square kilometers. The boundaries of the U.S. and the Soviet Union are less than 4 miles apart at one point in the Bering Strait.

Climate varies widely throughout the Soviet Union, where weather is similar to that in the United States, though on the whole somewhat cooler. About one-third of the land area is permafrost. Moscow, as well as other large cities such as Leningrad and Kiev, has four distinct seasons. Moscow lies at about the same latitude as Anchorage, Alaska. Summers are warm, sometimes exceeding 90°F (68°C), and often humid. Winters are cold and snowy, and early spring and late autumn can be wet and slushy, so waterproof boots or galoshes are a must nearly half the year.

GETTING TO MOSCOW

SOVIET VISAS

Business travelers to the Soviet Union (and accompanying spouses) must apply for a Soviet entry-exit business visa. To obtain a Soviet visa you must do two things: 1. Send the information needed by your sponsoring organization in the Soviet Union to enable it to obtain support for your Soviet visa, and 2. Complete a visa application and send it with the accompanying materials to the nearest Soviet Consulate (addresses on page 25-27).

Obtaining Soviet Visa Sponsorship. Each traveler (including spouses) must receive visa support from a sponsoring Soviet organization. This is usually done by first sending a telex or fax to the sponsoring Soviet organization in the Soviet Union asking for visa sponsorship confirmation. Your telex or fax requesting visa support should include your full name, date of birth, place of birth, citizenship, passport number, the date your passport was issued and the date it will expire, proposed dates of travel in the U.S.S.R., the names of the cities you will visit in the U.S.S.R., and the reason for your travel. Your Soviet sponsor's response and support confirmation (by telex or fax) should be submitted with your visa application to the Soviet Consulate.

The Visa Application. Carefully complete the Soviet visa application form and submit it to the nearest Soviet Consulate. Most experienced travel agents have these forms available and should be familiar with the submission procedure. Applications can also be obtained by contacting the Soviet Consulate. Travel arrangements should be made prior to submitting the visa application.

Visa applications must be accompanied by three identical 1½" by 1¾" photos, the visa application fee (it varies, so call ahead and ask the amount due), and photocopies of pages two and three of your U.S. passport. All passports must be valid for at least one month following the planned date of departure from the Soviet Union.

The visa application and supporting materials should be submitted to the Soviet Consulate at least three weeks prior to the anticipated date of departure from the United States. Also, if there is any chance that you may need to extend your stay in the Soviet Union, you might consider allowing for such possibilities on your application (i.e., extend your intended date of departure from the Soviet Union — it's easier to leave earlier than to have to make visa arrangements to stay longer than expected).

Your visa will not be stamped into your passport; it is a separate document to which your photograph is attached. Part of this document will be taken from you by an Immigration Officer when you arrive in the U.S.S.R., and the remaining part will be removed upon your departure. You will have no souvenir of your visa unless you make a photocopy of it.

Business visas for travel to the Soviet Union (except in rare instances) are issued for a single entry and exit, and they are valid for travel only to the Soviet cities listed. If, after arrival in Moscow, you find you must travel to another city in the U.S.S.R., you will need the assistance of your host organization to arrange permission for such travel.

Immunizations. Travelers should also check with the U.S. Public Health Service, Foreign Immunization Clinic, to determine what vaccinations are required or recommended for travel to the U.S.S.R. at a particular time. Generally speaking, no immunizations are required except for travelers to the Central Asian Republics, where gamma globulin and precautions against tetanus, diphtheria, polio, and typhoid are recommended.

SOVIET DIPLOMATIC OFFICES

Soviet Diplomatic Offices in the U.S. The offices of the U.S.S.R. Consulates in the U.S. are located at the following addresses.

Consulate of the U.S.S.R.
1825 Phelps Place, N.W.
Washington, D.C. 20008
Tel: (202) 939-8918
(between 9:00 AM
  and 12:00 PM)

Consulate of the U.S.S.R.
2790 Green Street
San Francisco, CA 94123
Tel: (415) 922-6642

Although it is not a diplomatic mission, the New York office of the Soviet travel organization Intourist may be of assistance to you or your travel agent in planning your trip. The address is: Intourist, 630 Fifth Ave., Suite 868, New York, NY 10020; Tel.: (212) 757-3884.

Soviet Diplomatic Offices in Selected Countries. The following is a list of Soviet Embassies, Consulates, and trade offices in various countries.

Austria

Die Botschast der UdSSR
  in Österreich
Reisnerstrasse 45-47
A-1030 Wien
Austria
Tel.: (43-1) 72-12-29
Telex: (47) 136278

Handelsvertretung der
  UdSSR in Österreich
Argentineerstrasse 25-27
Wien
Austria
Tel.: (43-1) 65-65-90
Telex: (47) 131848

Belgium

Soviet Embassy
  in Belgium
Avenue de Fré 66
1180 Brussels
Belgium
Tel.: (02) 374-3406

Soviet Consulate in
  Belgium
Rue Robert Jones 78
1189 Brussels
Belgium
Tel.: (02) 374-3569

Canada

Soviet Embassy in Canada
285 Charlotte Street
Ottawa, Ontario
K1N 8L5
Canada
Tel.: (613) 236-7220, 236-6215
Telex: 0533332
Fax: (613) 236-6342

Soviet Consulate
  in Canada
52 Range Road
Ottawa, Ontario
K1M 8J5
Tel.: (613) 236-7220
Telex: 0533396

Finland
Soviet Embassy in Finland
Tehtaankatu 1C
Helsinki
Finland
Tel.: 90-661876

France
Soviet Embassy in France
40-50 Boulevard Lannes
75116 Paris
France
Tel.: (33-1) 4504-0550
Telex: (42) 611761
Fax: (33-1) 4504-1765

Representation Commer-
 ciale de l'URSS en France
49 Rue de la Faisanderie
75116 Paris
France
Tel.: (33-1) 727-4139
Telex: (42) 611016

Germany (FRG)
Soviet Embassy in Germany
5300 Bonn 2
Waldstrasse 42
Postfach 200908
Federal Republic
 of Germany
Tel.: (49-228) 312085
Fax: (49-228) 384561

Handelsvertretung der
 UdSSR in BRD
5000 Köln 41
Friedrich-Engels-Strasse
Federal Republic
 of Germany
Tel.: (49-221) 431347
Telex: (41) 8881698

Italy
Soviet Embassy in Italy
Via Gaeta 5
00185 Rome
Italy
Tel.: (39-6) 494-1681
Telex: (43) 610237

Rappresentanza Commer-
 ciale dell'URSS in Italia
Via Clitunno, 46
00198 Rome
Italy
Tel.: (39-6) 844-3051
Telex: (43) 61023

Japan
Embassy of the USSR
1-1, Azabudai 2-chome
Minato-ku, Tokyo
Japan
Tel.: (03) 583-4224

Trade Representation
 of the U.S.S.R.
4-6-9, Takanawa
Minato-ku, Tokyo
Japan
Tel.: (03) 447-3291

Netherlands
Soviet Embassy
 in the Netherlands
Anton Bicker Weg 2
1079 RA Amsterdam
Tel.: (020) 45-13-00

Spain
Soviet Embassy
   in Spain
Madrid 6
C. Maestro Ripoll 14
Spain
Tel.: (34-1) 411-0707
Telex: (52) 45632

Delegación Comercial
   de la URSS
Avda. Comandante
   Franco, 30
Madrid 260-16
Spain
Tel.: (34-1) 250-1788
Telex: (52) 23830

Sweden
Soviet Embassy in Sweden
Gjörwellsgatan 31
S-112 60 Stockholm
Sweden
Tel.: 08/13 04 40

Consulate General
   of the Soviet Union
St. Sigfridsgaten #1
Göteborg
Sweden
Tel.: 031/40 80 84

United Kingdom
Soviet Embassy
   in the United Kindom
13 Kensington Palace
   Gardens
London W8
England
Tel.: (44-1) 228-3628
Telex: (51) 261420

Trade Delegation of
   the U.S.S.R. in the
   United Kingdom
32 Highgate West Hill
Westfield
London N6
England
Tel.: (44-1) 340-4492
Telex: 28577

ESSENTIALS TO PACK

Unless they are burdened with documentation or
samples, business visitors are sometimes able to pack all
their needs into carry-on baggage. This greatly reduces
baggage handling hassles (a one-hour wait at the

baggage pick-up area for checked baggage is the norm) and customs procedures on arrival in the Soviet Union, and is therefore recommended.

There are a few items that you should take to make yourself more comfortable during the flight. A bottle of drinking water will help counteract the dry air on the plane. Earplugs, eye shades, and slippers or comfortable shoes will aid your sleep during the flight, and will be useful during your stay as well.

While you should try to keep your baggage to a minimum, keep in mind that many items that you take for granted at home will not be available (or readily available) in the Soviet Union. Take along all personal hygiene supplies that may be needed; even when available, the Soviet equivalents are often not familiar or pleasing to Americans. Even such basics as soap, shampoo, sewing kits, towels and toilet paper may be absent from your hotel room.

Be sure to bring all the medical supplies that you will need, including refills of prescriptions, aspirin, vitamins, Dramamine, Lomotil, or other common medications that are not always available overseas. If you wear glasses or contact lenses, it is advisable to bring an extra pair and to carry your prescription with you.

In addition to toiletries and medical supplies, pack such items as film, blank audiocassettes, videotapes and batteries. These products, which are so readily available elsewhere, are not always available in the Soviet Union; when they are, they are considerably more expensive.

AIR CONNECTIONS WITH MOSCOW

Routes. There are many ways to reach Moscow by air, whether you are departing from the U.S. or Europe.

Flights Between the U.S. and Moscow. As of mid-1990, both Pan Am (Pan Am Bldg., New York, NY 10166; 212-687-2600) and Aeroflot (630 Fifth Ave., New York, NY 10111; 212-397-1660) offered nonstop service between the U.S. and the U.S.S.R. Nonstop flights operate five days per week between New York's JFK airport and Moscow. Departures from New York are in the evening with arrival in Moscow the following morning. Nonstop flying time from New York to Moscow is about 9½ hours.

At the time of publication, approximate round-trip airfares for the New York–Moscow trip were as follows:

Budget (APEX)	$1,000
Excursion	$1,600
Economy (nonrestricted)	$2,060
Business class	$2,646
First class	$4,312

Pan Am, together with several European airlines, offers direct connections between New York and Moscow via some European cities. Good connections are available through Finnair, KLM, Scandinavian, and Air France, among others. Pan Am's flight currently operates three days per week, with departures from New York in the evening. A typical flight time for a one-stop trip is 14½ hours. Aeroflot also offers connecting flights from New York to Moscow with stops at Gander, Newfoundland, and Shannon, Ireland. There currently are five flights per week, with departures in late afternoon and arrivals in Moscow early the following afternoon.

Aeroflot currently operates three flights per week between Washington's Dulles Airport and Moscow, with a one-hour refueling stop in Gander, Newfoundland. Total flight time (including the stop at Gander) is 11 hours. Airfares from Washington, D.C. to Moscow are slightly higher than those listed for New York to Moscow.

Aeroflot's reputation for less-than-appetizing inflight meals is changing as a result of a catering joint venture between Aeroflot and the Marriott Corporation, AEROMAR, Ltd.

Because airline routes and schedules are always changing, your travel agent is probably in the best position to advise you about travel to Moscow.

Moscow to the U.S. There are nonstop flights from Moscow to New York five days per week, with departures from Moscow at midday and arrivals at JFK in the late afternoon. The trip is about 10½ hours, somewhat longer than from New York to Moscow because of the jet stream. There are also several connecting flights from Moscow to New York.

Other Routes. There are, of course, other ways to reach Moscow by air. Travelers originating from other large U.S. cities or Europe may prefer to fly through Frankfurt, Paris, London or Helsinki, depending on the international airline services available to them.

Fighting Jet Lag

Because business trips are often brief, with meetings and other demands beginning shortly after arrival, jet lag can be a major problem for the business traveler.

There are several things that can be done to minimize jet lag. Before the trip, ask your travel agent about the flight menu, and order the lightest, most healthful meal possible. Things to avoid are: greasy, fatty foods (e.g., red meat, gravies, sauces, cheese, and nuts); foods that are high in sodium (they cause water retention, which leads to swollen hands and feet — a real discomfort when you are essentially immobilized on a long flight); desserts (except fruits); alcohol and coffee (they are diuretics and will dehydrate you — however, if you feel you must have them, drink four times the amount in water); and carbonated sodas, especially diet sodas (the carbonation can expand in your stomach as you gain altitude, causing discomfort — and they're also high in sodium).

Try to relax and rest during the flight. Read, listen to soothing music, and sleep (your eye shades and earplugs will help facilitate this). Although space is limited on the plane, you can walk a bit and do some stretching and flexing exercises in your seat.

SOVIET CUSTOMS REGULATIONS AND PROCEDURES

Business travelers to the Soviet Union should familiarize themselves with Soviet customs regulations, which are available from the Amtorg Trading Corporation and the U.S.S.R. Trade Representation.

Amtorg Trading Corporation
1755 Broadway
New York, NY 10019
Tel: (212) 956-3010

U.S.S.R. Trade
    Representation
2001 Connecticut
    Ave., N.W.
Washington, D.C. 20008
Tel: (202) 232-5988

Arrival. Certain printed matter may be confiscated if Soviet officials feel it is political in nature, especially publications dealing with internal conditions in the U.S.S.R. Anyone discovered carrying contraband material risks detention or denial of permission to enter the U.S.S.R.

Soviet law permits product samples to be brought into the U.S.S.R. duty-free. If you are bringing samples, it may help to have documentation from the intended Soviet recipient explaining that you have been requested to bring certain specified samples. Otherwise, the examining customs officer may charge you a substantial duty.

Customs Declaration Forms. The Soviet customs declaration is a record of the currency and other valuables you have in your possession when you enter the country. Precious metals and jewelry must be listed on it. Rings, watches, and such valuables as cameras and calculators are not specified, but some customs officers may direct you to list such items. It is essential that you fill out the declaration correctly and possess it at all times. Accurate records, especially in regard to currency regulations, are important.

A Two-Channel Arrival System. Soviet customs authorities have developed a simplified system for arriving international passengers. The system consists of two channels: a green channel for passengers with nothing to declare and with less than $50.00 (or the equivalent); and a red channel for all other passengers. While delays at the customs checkpoint have been ameliorated by this system, Soviet customs officials are very thorough, particularly when examining luggage. If you travel with a great deal of luggage, more than $50.00 (or the equivalent) or unusually large amounts of items that are valuable or scarce in the Soviet Union (e.g., books about the Soviet Union, audiocassettes, cameras, videocameras, film and jewelry), you will be directed to the red channel. There, luggage will be painstakingly examined, and you may be delayed if questions arise over whether you can proceed with your belongings. This process can delay you for at least one hour. Add to that an hour or so spent waiting for your luggage at the baggage pickup area, and you may waste a total of two aggravating hours at the airport.

If, on the other hand, you have carry-on luggage only, and have not packed an unusual amount of valuable items or books that might be confiscated, or more than $50.00 (or the equivalent), you can proceed through the green channel with relative ease and speed. Barring unusual delays at the immigration checkpoint (where your visa will be checked), you can generally expect to get from the plane through immigration and into a taxi in 30 minutes or less.

Departure. When leaving the Soviet Union, be sure to arrive at the airport no less than two hours before your flight departs. Exit procedures are maddeningly inefficient. There is no two-channel system for departing passengers, and you will find yourself on long lines amid many emigrating Soviet nationals who are usually heavily laden with luggage. You must wait on line at Customs, and then rush to get on line at the flight check-in point (which often isn't available until one hour before departure). Finally, you must pass through the immigration exit procedure (where the remainder of your visa is surrendered).

Remember that in addition to presenting your customs declaration form to Soviet officials when arriving in the U.S.S.R., you must also complete a second declaration, for departure purposes. Both forms must be presented to the customs officer on departure. Furthermore, when you present the customs declaration that was stamped when you arrived, together with a departure customs form, any valuables that appear on one but not on the other may be heavily taxed or confiscated.

YOUR MOSCOW STAY

SOVIET TOURIST ORGANIZATIONS

Intourist is the major travel agency in the Soviet Union. It gets you into hotels and restaurants, in virtual monopolist style, and deals with all aspects of foreign travel. Intourist provides English-speaking guides for general (group) and custom (individual) sightseeing. In Moscow, the Intourist office is located at 16 Marx Prospect (tel.: 203-6962).

There are two other travel agencies in the U.S.S.R.: **Interbureau**, the Tourist Council of the Trade Unions, which, as you might guess, organizes travel by trade union representatives and also deals with all types of individual tourism. The third travel bureau is **Sputnik Travel Agency**, located at 4 Lebyazhy Pereulok (phone number: 223-9512). It organizes group tours for students and young people and accommodates them in tourist class hotels.

HOTEL ACCOMMODATIONS

In its effort to attract more foreign visitors and earn more foreign exchange, the Soviet government, with the help of foreign partners, has begun renovating and upgrading hotels in virtually every major Soviet city. In 1989, the Savoy Hotel (formerly the Berlin) reopened as Moscow's first Western-style luxury hotel, now resplendant with a stylish bar, a gambling casino and 24-hour viewing of Cable News Network on TV sets in every room. Other hotels, like the Metropole, which is currently being refurbished, and the National, which is slated for renovation, are expected to rival the Savoy in their elegance and services.

Visitors must stay in hotels pre-assigned to them by Intourist, the government travel agency, or arranged by a Soviet host organization or a travel agent. You can ask for a hotel on a list provided by Intourist, but you will not always receive your first choice. The current shortage of hotel rooms in Moscow makes it difficult to switch hotels. The two classes of tourist accommodations — deluxe (more than $200 for two-room suites and over $300 for three- or four-room suites per night) and first class (over $125 for a single room per night) — fall short of the standards of even moderately priced hotels in Western Europe and the U.S. Payment in hard currency is obligatory.

Unless you are staying at one of Moscow's two or three leading hotels, you will find conditions rather spartan. Considering that you will probably pay $100 a day, you may feel doubly uncomfortable. The beds are small, cot-like and low to the floor. There might be a writing table, but you will look in vain for stationery or postcards, or ready information on laundry or dry cleaning services.

Towels are small and coarse. Lighting is poor. There
might be a television in the room, but unless you understand Russian you'll be unable to comprehend more than
an exercise show or music or a dance program. Electric
power, outlets and electrical fixtures are not always reliable, so it's not a good idea to depend on appliances like
an electric razor, or hair dryers. Hot water may not be
available throughout the day, and if it is available at the
peak hour for morning showers, the water pressure may
be weak. Bathroom tissue is on the rough side, and many
sinks and baths do not have rubber stoppers — flat
rubber stoppers are essential items to pack if you plan
to take a tub bath or wash your own clothes. If you prefer
room service dining, bring your own food. And, as the
dezhurnaya (the hotel employee, invariably a woman,
who sits at a desk near the elevator) may sternly remind
you, remember to turn out all lights and unplug the television when you leave the room.

Checking In. When checking into a hotel, you must
present an Intourist voucher (unless other payment
arrangements have been made) and leave your passport
with the reception desk for at least one day. You will be
issued a hotel pass *(propusk)*, which must be presented
to gain admission to the hotel. The *propusk* contains your
name, the name and address of the hotel, and some information about hotel services. In many hotels, you are
supposed to give your key to a *dezhurnaya* when leaving
your room. If you're lucky, the *dezhurnaya* will hold your
messages and mail, call taxis for you and place telephone
calls abroad. Give yourself plenty of time for long
distance calls; it can sometimes take more than 12 hours
to reach phone numbers abroad. Some nights it is simply
impossible to get through.

Doormen tend to be indifferent, although some will
assist with luggage. All will check for your *propusk*.
Many hotel lobbies are populated by Soviet "mafia"
types, black marketeers, and prostitutes seeking your
attention and money. Some dealers will invite you to a
room, perhaps to show you an "antique" samovar or a
Soviet Red Army watch (which they have mysteriously
and illegally obtained). It can be risky to deal with these
people; they are watched closely by the authorities. Most
hotels include *beryozkas*, special stores that sell Soviet
and Western souvenirs, clothing, books, music, food and
liquor, all available for foreign currency only. In addition,

each hotel has service bureaus with English-speaking employees who can provide you with rental cars, tours, and entertainment bookings.

Each Intourist hotel has at least one large restaurant, and many of them offer a nightly entertainment show, usually featuring traditional Russian dance and song. These evenings are also attended by jovial guests, and they can resemble wedding receptions with their boisterous and jubilant atmosphere, fueled, of course, by the flow of vodka and champagne toasts. The quality of the food varies from hotel to hotel, and reservations are essential. Some hotels include restaurants for foreigners only, with payment required in hard currency.

Selected Moscow Hotels

In Moscow, Western tourists usually stay in one of the eight hotels described below. Most, except for the Cosmos, are located near the center of the city. They are listed from best to worst according to overall atmosphere, room standards, quality of service, and location.

Savoy, 3 Zhdanov Street, 03368 (tel.: 225-6910)

The best hotel in the Soviet Union, in a league of its own. Built in 1912, the Savoy was renovated by the Yugoslavs and reopened in 1989 as the first Western-style luxury hotel in the country. A joint venture between Intourist and Finnair manages the hotel, which contains only 155 beds and 86 rooms (only 18 singles), each with a different decor. In 1990, singles cost $186, doubles $232, deluxe rooms $312, and suites $416 and up, per night. Reservations are virtually impossible to get unless you fly to Moscow first class or business class and make your hotel and air travel reservations together.

The hotel features a gambling casino, a small *beryozka,* and laundry, dry cleaning, and limousine services, as well as round-the-clock CNN television broadcasts and a refrigerator bar in every room. The Savoy's main bar is ideal for a nightcap and also serves tasty dishes. The pricey but excellent restaurant in the basement of the hotel has slow service but is unrivaled in its ambience and selections. Selections on the room service menu are also excellent, especially the "West Coast salad" and the *blini* (pancakes) with caviar. Copying and fax machines are available. *USA Today* is sold in the lobby.

The Savoy has an excellent location, across the street from the famous children's department store, Detsky Mir, just off Marx Prospect and only a short walk to the Bolshoi Ballet and Red Square.

Metropol, 1 Marx Prospect, 103012 (tel.: 225-6677)

Expected to reopen in July 1990, after a four-year Finnish renovation. Intourist claims it will be superior even to the Savoy, billing it as no less than "the best in Europe."

The Metropol will reopen with 766 beds, 402 rooms (ranging from $159 for singles to $585 for a four-room suite, per night) and seating space for more than 1,500 people in its various restaurants, cafés, and bars. This Intourist-run hotel will also feature an authentic Russian tea room, swimming pool, gym, beauty salon, conference hall, laundry, dry cleaning, fax and copying services as well as an underground garage and numerous boutiques and kiosks.

Initially built between 1899 and 1903, the building itself is a historic landmark frequented by Lenin and other revolutionaries for private meetings and public gatherings. The Metropol is ideally located in the heart of Sverdlov Square, diagonally across from the Bolshoi and only a stone's — or better, a rose's — throw away.

Mezhdunarodnaya (Russian for the "International"), 12 Krasnopresnenskaya Embankment, 123610 (tel.: 253-7729, telex 411486)

Known simply as the "Mezh," this non-Intourist hotel caters mainly to business visitors and special delegations. Built in 1980 as part of a three-building complex known as the International Trade Center, the 22-story, ultramodern hotel is managed by Sovincentr, an affiliate of the U.S.S.R. Chamber of Commerce. It resembles many atrium-type Hyatt hotels, with its glass elevators and indoor terraces. The Mezh, which consists of 450 rooms (more than $125 for singles per night), offers an array of 250 services and conveniences, including a travel bureau, health club, bowling alley, swimming pool, sauna, various boutiques, a supermarket filled with Western goods, dry cleaning and laundry, underground parking as well as copying and fax machines. It also has several restaurants and pubs, including a German beer hall and an authentic and very expensive Japanese restaurant replete with *sushi* bar. A popular attraction is the lobby centerpiece, a mechanical rooster clock that crows on the hour. Despite its relatively central location, the Mezh is not close to any metro station. Taxis — except in foul weather — are plentiful.

National, 14/1 Marx Prospect, 103009 (tel.: 203-6539)

Also a historic landmark, the National is situated directly across from the Kremlin and Red Square. Originally built in 1903, and later expanded in the 1960's, this charming hotel is scheduled for a facelift as soon as the new Metropol is completed. Many of its 199 rooms, ranging from $146 to $354 per night, are elegantly furnished with antiques. A small, but well-stocked *beryozka* as well as a Kodak film shop are located in the narrow lobby, just in front of the beautiful, art-deco staircase that leads up to the hotel's excellent restaurants and bars. Lenin and his wife, Krupskaya, lived in a second-floor room that faces the Kremlin. This room, number 107, is now the hotel manager's office, but still contains some of the former leader's personal effects and furniture, including his desk. *USA Today* is sold in the lobby and fax machines are also available.

Intourist, 3,5 Gorky Street, 103600 (tel.: 203-4008, telex 411823)

Lacking the charm of its next-door neighbor, the National Hotel, this 22-floor rectangular block has an excellent location on Moscow's main street, equidistant from Lenin's Tomb in Red Square and the now obligatory McDonald's — about a 10-minute walk from each. It is Moscow's main Intourist service center. The hotel, which opened in 1970, has slot machines and several bars and restaurants, including an inexpensive, all-you-can-eat buffet for breakfast and lunch every day, as well as a tasty Chinese café on the 10th floor.

The Intourist's 458 rooms, which range from $128 for singles to $315 for three-room suites per night, are plain and uninviting.

Rossiya, 6 Razin Street, near Red Square (tel.: 298-5400)

This gigantic hotel, the largest in the Soviet Union and certainly one of the largest in the world, can accommodate 6,000 guests in its 3,150 rooms (from $128 for singles to $315 for three-room suites per night). Walls are thin, halls are noisy, and the rooms are dowdy.

This drab, chrome-and-glass hotel was built in 1967 to commemorate the 50th anniversary of the Bolshevik Revolution. The Rossiya is best known for its huge *beryozka,* the largest in Moscow, and its panoramic views from behind St. Basil's Cathedral.

The labyrinthine hotel has four separate entrances, two cinemas, a 3,000-seat concert hall, over 20 bars and cafés, and a well-known 21st-floor restaurant that offers a breathtaking view of the city. Baskin and Robbins ice cream and *USA Today* are sold on the ground floor.

Ukraina, 2/1 Kutuzovsky Prospect (tel.: 243-3021)

Another landmark hotel located on the banks of the Moskva River. Built in the 1930's in the vogue of Stalinist neo-gothic architecture, this 29-story hotel has 1,500 unadorned rooms, ranging from $125 for singles to $205 for a two-room suite. It is identical to six other buildings in Moscow (including Moscow State University and the Foreign Ministry) and bears a resemblance to the well-known building from the American movie, *Ghostbusters.* The Victorian-looking lobby contains a well-supplied *beryozka* and a large restaurant. Limousine, laundry and dry-cleaning services are offered.

The Ukraina is only a few minutes from the center of the city. The Mezhdunarodnaya Hotel and other buildings in the International Trade Center complex are across the river, and the historic Arbat district and the busy Kalinin Prospect are nearby. So, too, are the Ministry of Foreign Trade and the U.S. Embassy. In a management joint venture, Pan American World Airways and Aeroflot sell three floors of rooms to businessmen and travel groups.

Cosmos, 150 Mira Prospect, 129366 (tel.: 217-0785)

Another mammouth hotel with 3,534 beds and 1,767 rooms, including 56 suites ($315 per night) and the rest doubles ($146 per night). Completed in 1979 for the 1980 Moscow Summer Olympic Games, the 26-story, French-built hotel features a bowling alley, swimming pool, sauna, masseur, small *beryozka,* three large restaurants, four bars, and an all-you-can-eat buffet every day at lunch. Fax machines are available.

The semicircular building is at least 15–20 minutes from the center of Moscow, but it stands next to a metro station and taxis are available. Near the hotel stand several famous statues as well as the huge Exhibition of Economic Achievements. Recently, the Cosmos has acquired a seedy reputation because of the many prostitutes and black marketeers that inhabit its lobby.

FOOD AND RESTAURANTS

Foreign visitors complain about their meals more than anything else in the Soviet Union. Experienced travelers to Moscow often stuff their suitcases with as much food as clothing. However, if you know the ropes, it is possible to find a decent meal in Moscow.

The number and variety of restaurants have been growing over the last few years with the emergence of private, or cooperative, restaurants. Cooperatives cost quite a bit more than state-run restaurants, but they serve some of the best food in the city. Still, most agree that no restaurant meal can top home-cooked Russian fare.

While it is a good idea to pack granola bars, canned tuna and canned fruit, Moscow's restaurants should be sampled, if only for a cultural experience or a good laugh (for example, try forcing down a typical Moscow breakfast of sardines, pickled garlic cloves and beef tongue).

One of the most annoying aspects of eating in the Soviet Union is that it is difficult to find quick meals or snacks on the spur of the moment. Early reservations are necessary for almost every restaurant, and service is agonizingly slow. Almost every well-known restaurant is guarded by immovable doormen who insist that the place is full even when empty tables are visible.

Moscow's restaurants offer diverse menus, with many specializing in the cuisines of the Soviet Union's different republics. Georgian and Uzbek restaurants are recommended for their flavorful, often spicy dishes like *satsivi* (chicken in walnut sauce), *plof* (rice with diced lamb, chicken, pork or beef) and *shashlik* (grilled pork or beef on skewers).

When you sit down to lunch or dinner in a Russian restaurant, you usually are greeted by an assortment of *zakuski*, or hors d'oeuvres, including red or black caviar (*ikra*), marinated vegetables and platters of cold meat and fish and the ubiquitous cucumbers. Ask for mushrooms julienne, a tasty mixture of sliced mushrooms in sour cream and hot melted cheese. Also try *pelmeni*, Siberian-style meat dumplings, and borscht, a red beet and vegetable soup served with stewed meat and a dollop of sour cream. If all else fails, fill up on the coarse, but often tasty white and black breads. If you enjoy your meal, tell the waiter it was delicious, or *vkysna* (VKOOS-nah).

No food seems to tickle the Soviet palate more than ice cream, or *morozhanaya* (mah-ROW-jah-nye-yah). Even in sub-zero temperatures, it is not uncommon to see long lines at outdoor ice cream stands. The product hardly compares to Ben and Jerry's or Baskin and Robbins, but it may be one the few Moscow food items you will eat without hesitation. Some of the best ice cream sundaes are served at Cosmos at 4 Gorky Street (tel.: 295-6544).

Moscow's produce markets are another gastronomical attraction. Known as *rynoks* (pronounced RY nuhk), these markets sell startlingly fresh meat, vegetables and fruit grown privately by farmers from various regions of the country. Prices there are substantially higher than those in state stores. Bring a Soviet friend along to bargain for you. The Tsentralnyi Rynok (Central Market) at 15 Tsvetnoy Boulevard is the largest, but most expensive.

Beverages are hard to come by throughout the U.S.S.R. Mineral water and Pepsi are the most commonly available non-alcoholic drinks (tap water tastes awful and is of questionable purity). Georgian wines, especially the dry whites (Gurdzhani is the best) and reds (Mukuzani is recommended), may pleasantly surprise you. Several brands of Soviet vodka can be found in most restaurants. Stolichnaya, the U.S.S.R.'s best known vodka, is cheaper outside than inside the Soviet Union. Soviet champagne is drinkable, but exceedingly sweet. The more adventurous should try *kvas*, the Russian version of beer. It is sold from communal cups in machines on the street (you should probably bring your own glass).

Some state-owned restaurants still offer the best menus and prices. For example, a meal of steak, french fries, vodka and salad costs only 5 to 8 rubles (85 cents to $1.30) in a state-run restaurant, while the same meal costs as much as 30 to 40 rubles ($5 to $6.50) in a cooperative restaurant. To avoid being cheated, ask about prices when you order; sometimes prices are not listed on menus and are arbitrarily decided at the end of your meal by the restaurant's owners or managers. Your meals may be cheaper when you dine with Soviets. Like taxis, cooperatives may not seat you unless you pay in *voluta,* or foreign currency.

Western food establishments, like the recently opened **McDonald's**, near Pushkin Square, and **Nathan's** hot dog stand (*voluta* only), in front of the Mezhdunarodnaya Hotel, are gradually arriving on the scene. A Pizza Hut is under construction on Gorky Street. Moscow also has a few Chinese restaurants, but none that compare to the quality of Chinese food commonly found in the West. **Mi-Hud** (tel.: 264-9574), a new cooperative restaurant near Three Stations Square, serves the best Chinese food in the city. **Sakura** (see below), the lone Japanese restaurant, looks and tastes authentic, especially with its *sushi* bar. Unfortunately, its high prices may shock you. Another new cooperative called **Lasagna** (tel.: 231-1085) prepares Italian dishes, including homemade pasta. The **Olimp** has a most lavish Paris-style floor show. **Delhi** (23 Krasnaya Presnaya, tel.: 252-1760), an Indian restaurant opened in 1988 by a Soviet-Indian joint venture, is recommended for its unique-tasting Indian food, intimate atmosphere and entertainment of Indian dance.

All hotels contain at least one restaurant that offers elaborate entertainment programs and dancing. Full meal prices range from as little as 5 rubles a head in state-owned restaurants to more than 90 rubles in cooperatives. Tips are not required in any restaurants, but few waiters will refuse them. Incidentally, the cheapest way to buy vodka or caviar in Moscow is to subtly ask a waiter or restaurant employee to sell you some. The only other place to buy caviar and vodka is in *beryozkas,* where they are offered at much higher prices.

Bars, as we know them in the West, are few and far between in Moscow. The elegant one in the Savoy Hotel, which only accepts foreign currency and does not permit Soviet citizens, is popular for its large selection, delicious menu, American television programming and old-fashioned decor. The National Hotel's second-floor, foreign-currency bar is often frequented for nightcaps. The **Sinyaya Ptitsa** ("Blue Bird," tel.: 299-8702), at 23 Chekhov Street, is Moscow's token jazz club.

Selected Moscow Restaurants

It is difficult to rate Moscow's restaurants, because the quality of their food can change dramatically from night to night. What follows is a list, in alphabetical order, of 10 of Moscow's more popular restaurants.

Aragvi, 6 Gorky Street (tel.: 229-3762). One of Moscow's best known Georgian restaurants, located in the heart of the city. Named after a famous river in Georgia, the food in this state-owned restaurant gets mixed reviews. Once a favorite of Winston Churchill's, Aragvi includes among its specialties *lavash* (Georgian bread), *lobio* (beans in a spicy sauce), *kharcho* (spicy meat soup), chicken *satsivi* and *shashlik*. It also offers a large selection of Georgian wines and brandies. Stories from Georgian history are painted on the restaurant's walls. Prices are reasonable — a full meal with vodka and wine costs about only 14 rubles a head. Reservations are essential, but difficult to get. Many tables are reserved for Soviet VIP's. Private rooms are available for small parties and banquets. Rubles are accepted.

Baku, 24 Gorky Street (tel.: 299-9426). Excellent Azerbaijani food and music. A state-run restaurant known for its varieties of *plof.* Also try *dovta* (sour milk and meat soup) and *narkurma* (roast lamb with pomegranate seeds). Rubles are accepted.

Cooperative Skazka ("Fairy Tale"), 1 Tovarishchesky Pereulok. New, highly touted cooperative restaurant near the Taganka Theater. Interior is cramped and dark, and tables are small. Former U.S. Secretary of State George Shultz ate here during a visit to Moscow (his autographed photo is on the wall near the entrance). Reservations are virtually impossible to obtain unless you agree to pay in foreign currency. The menu is extensive but prices are high. The entertainment mixes folk music with dixieland. Don't confuse this restaurant with

two others of the same name, one in the Intourist Hotel
and the other on the Yaroslavskoyo Shosse.

Cooperative Taganka. Popular with foreign residents
in Moscow, this cooperative restaurant offers an attractive display of appetizers — but be forewarned that they
do not taste as good as they look. The restaurant's best
offering is its table-side entertainment. Prices are not
listed on the menu, and may vary according to the whims
of the restaurant's owners and managers. Insist on
paying for your meal in rubles. There is a 5-ruble cover
charge for entertainment. Tables are small and the
interior is dark and cavernous. The location is good —
next to the Tanganka Theater and the Tanganskaya
metro station.

National Hotel, 1 Gorky Street (tel.: 203-5595), second
floor, fifth hall. One of Moscow's finest Russian restaurants, with a spectacular view of the Kremlin and Red
Square. A state-owned restaurant offering the classics
of Russian cuisine. Chicken Kiev and mushrooms
julienne are recommended. Its old-fashioned, elegant
interior has a small dance floor and live music at night.
Dinner with large platters of appetizers and choice of
entrees costs 30 rubles a head ($5). A late-night foreign-
currency bar is located on the same floor. Reservations
are difficult to get. Rubles are accepted.

Praga, 2 Arbat Street (tel.: 290-6171). Opened at the
turn-of-the-century, this state-owned restaurant specializes in Czech and Russian cuisine. An exclusive Soviet
VIP haunt with several dining rooms and a garden,
Praga is well-known for its Chicken Kiev and rich chocolate cream cake. Reservations are difficult to get. Rubles
are accepted and dinner costs about 30 to 40 rubles a
head. After dinner, take a walk along the Arbat, one of
Moscow's oldest and most famous streets.

Sakura, Hotel Mezhdunarodnaya, 12 Krasnopresnenskaya Embankment (tel.: 253-2894). Moscow's only
Japanese restaurant, opened in 1982. Small portions for
big money (at least $60 a head). Authentic interior, very
clean and modern, serving *sake* and *sushi*. Only foreign
currency is accepted.

Savoy Hotel, 3 Zhdanov Street (tel.: 223-3581). Moscow's most elegant and expensive restaurant, reopened in 1989. Gorgeous, old-fashioned decor. Service is painfully slow and the food is overpriced and overrated. The West Coast Salad (seafood and chopped vegetables with a vinaigrette dressing) and *blini* with caviar stand out. Only foreign currency is accepted. Reservations are essential, but not too difficult to obtain (given the prices and service).

Slavyansky Bazaar ("Slavic Fair"), 13 October 25th Street (tel.: 228-4845). The Soviet Union's oldest restaurant, which once catered to such Russian greats as Chekhov, Tolstoy, Tchaikovsky and Stanislavsky. A festive atmosphere is fed by a large stage featuring corny and noisy folk entertainment. This state-owned restaurant opened in 1870 after having been converted from a domed market building; it was restored in 1966 and offers traditional Russian cuisine at about 40 rubles a head. Reservations are required and difficult to get. Rubles are accepted. Private dining rooms are available.

Uzbekistan, 29 Neglinnaya Street (tel.: 294-6053). The best Uzbek restaurant in the city, specializing in *lagman* (spicy meat and noodle soup), *plof* and *shashlik*. Colorful atmosphere with live Uzbek music and entertainment.

GETTING AROUND MOSCOW

Depending on your mode of transport, getting around Moscow can be one of the most pleasant aspects of your stay, or the most frustrating. Virtually all street and metro signs are written in Russian so, unless you understand the language, it is not advisable to go from place to place on your own. Soviet citizens, in general, do not speak English, but will usually go out of their way to help foreigners find their destinations.

Taxis. It seems that almost everyone who owns a car in Moscow is also a cab driver. Meters exist, but are rarely used. Cabbies follow their own rules, setting fares arbitrarily. For this reason, they may turn out to be your Moscow nemesis.

46 GETTING AROUND MOSCOW

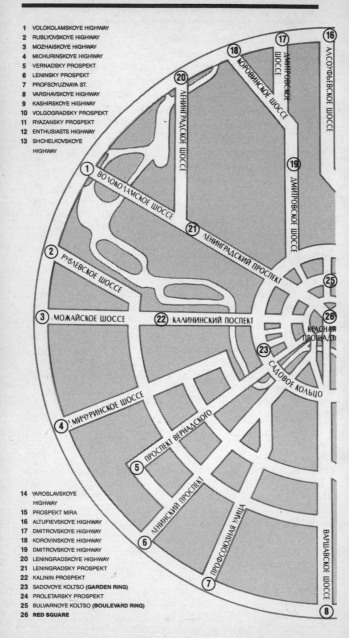

1 VOLOKOLAMSKOYE HIGHWAY
2 RUBLYOVSKOYE HIGHWAY
3 MOZHAISKOYE HIGHWAY
4 MICHURINSKOYE HIGHWAY
5 VERNADSKY PROSPEKT
6 LENINSKY PROSPEKT
7 PROFSOYUZNAYA ST.
8 VARSHAVSKOYE HIGHWAY
9 KASHIRSKOYE HIGHWAY
10 VOLGOGRADSKY PROSPEKT
11 RYAZANSKY PROSPEKT
12 ENTHUSIASTS HIGHWAY
13 SHCHELKOVSKOYE
   HIGHWAY

14 YAROSLAVSKOYE
   HIGHWAY
15 PROSPEKT MIRA
16 ALTUFIEVSKOYE HIGHWAY
17 DMITROVSKOYE HIGHWAY
18 KOROVINSKOYE HIGHWAY
19 DMITROVSKOYE HIGHWAY
20 LENINGRADSKOYE HIGHWAY
21 LENINGRADSKY PROSPEKT
22 KALININ PROSPEKT
23 SADOVOYE KOLTSO (GARDEN RING)
24 PROLETARSKY PROSPEKT
25 BULVARNOYE KOLTSO (BOULEVARD RING)
26 RED SQUARE

GREATER MOSCOW

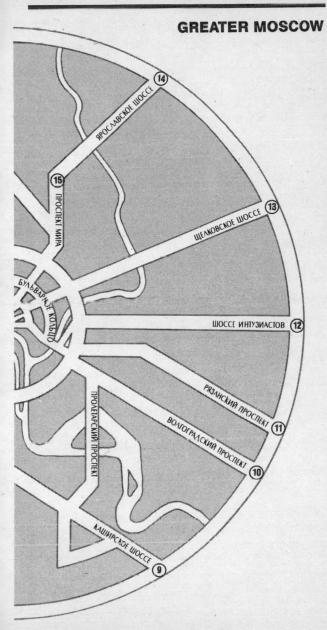

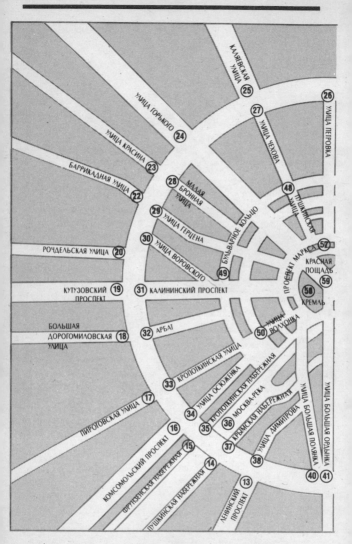

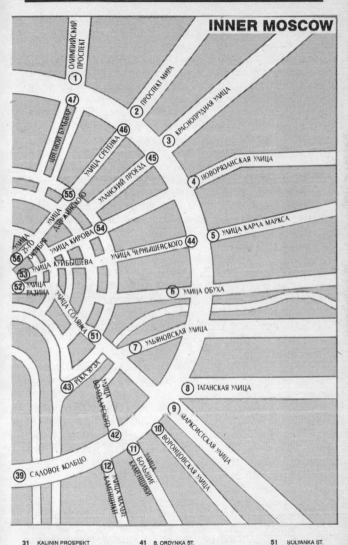

INNER MOSCOW

31	KALININ PROSPEKT	41	B. ORDYNKA ST.	51	SOLYANKA ST.
32	ARBAT ST.	42	VOLODARSKY ST.	52	RAZIN ST.
33	KROPOTKIN SKAYA ST.	43	YALIZA RIVER	53	KUIBYSHEV ST.
34	OSTO ZHENKA ST.	44	CHERNYSHEVSKY ST.	54	KIROV ST
35	KROPOTKINSKAYA EMBANKMENT	45	ULANSKY LANE	55	DZERZHINSKY ST.
36	MOSKVA RIVER	46	SRETENKA ST.	56	25TH OCT. ST.
37	KRYMSKAYA EMBANKMENT	47	TSVETNOY BOULEVARD	57	MARX PROSPEKT
38	DIMITROV ST.	48	PUSHKINSKAYA ST.	58	KREMLIN
39	SADOVOYE KOLTSO (GARDEN RING)	49	BULVARNOYE KOLTSO (BOULEVARD RING)	59	RED SQUARE
40	B. POLYANKA ST.	50	VOLKHONKA ST.		

Unlike cabbies in most large Western cities, Moscow's taxi drivers, when they are free, do not always pick up waving customers. Sometimes they may even refuse to stop. If they do stop, they always ask (in Russian, of course), "Where to?" (*Kuda vam yekhat?*) and "How much?" (*Skolka?*). If your offer is not high enough, they will refuse your business, saying they are not driving in your direction or that their shift is ending. Often that's a signal for you to up your offer. In the Soviet Union, you will find that offering the right amount of money will often get you anything you want or need.

It is crucial that you and your taxi driver agree to a fare before going anywhere. Resist paying in any currency but rubles. With the number of Western tourists increasing in Moscow, many cabbies now illegally demand that foreigners pay in U.S. dollars, Deutsche marks, or Western products such as cigarettes. Even the drivers of the 11,000 state-owned taxis customarily ignore their meters and demand fares 7 to 10 times higher than the meter rate, which is 20 kopeks (about 3 cents) per kilometer plus tip. Official taxis are usually yellow with a checkered design on their doors and a small green light on the upper right-hand corner of the windshield. When this light is on, the drivers are available, but that does not necessarily mean they will stop for you.

It is customary to share cabs with strangers. Whenever possible, try to travel in the company of Soviet citizens, who can negotiate a reasonable taxi fare for you. Cabbies usually charge lower fares for Soviet customers, and even use the meter for them. The 40-minute, 28-mile car ride from downtown to Sheremetyevo Airport (the largest of four airports near the city and the principal one for international flights) may cost tourists as much as 30 to 35 rubles ($5 to $6), but will cost only about 10 rubles — less than $2 — for Soviet passengers. Unless you are paying the meter rate, you will not be expected to tip the driver (in that case, the entire fare is in effect the tip). Many business visitors have discovered that cabbies are well satisfied with a carton of cigarettes for the trip between Moscow and Sheremetyevo.

Most taxi drivers speak only Russian, but they do try to strike up conversations with their foreign passengers. They sometimes try to prevent passengers from fastening their seat belts (if there are any), considering it an insult to their driving ability. Stick to your guns, because many do drive recklessly, setting the pell-mell pace of Moscow traffic. This danger only becomes worse in the winter, when a lack of snow tires and traction devices leaves drivers sliding and spinning along the city's's twisting, icy thoroughfares.

Metro (Subway). Moscow's widely acclaimed metro system is cheap, fast and reliable. Its system of nine color-coded lines and more than 130 stations reaches every region of the city. Trains ordinarily arrive at each station every two to four minutes and every 50 seconds during rush hours. The spotless stations resemble art museums with their colorful mosaics, large bronze statues and friezes. Even if you prefer to travel aboveground, you should visit such metro stations as Mayakovskaya and Ploschad Revolutsi, simply for their impressive sculpture and designs. For many foreigners, Moscow's metro system stands out as one of the Soviet Union's major technological achievements.

Perhaps the metro's only drawbacks are that it is often overcrowded and that its directional signs are only in Russian. Still, it is the best bargain in town, costing only 5 kopeks (less than a penny) regardless of the distance you travel. Metro stations operate Monday through Saturday from 6 AM to 1 AM and until 1:30 AM on Sundays. Automated change machines and metro maps are located at the entrance to each station. After you drop your 5 kopek coin into the turnstile slot, wait until the turnstile's white light turns orange before walking through it. Otherwise, you will be rudely obstructed by metal bars at knee and waist levels.

Almost all Westerners' hotels are located next to metro stops, which are marked by large illuminated "M" signs on the street level. It is not possible to reach any of Moscow's four airports by metro.

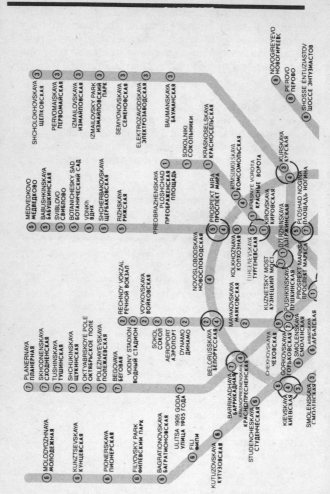

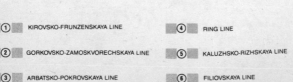

① KIROVSKO-FRUNZENSKAYA LINE

② GORKOVSKO-ZAMOSKVORECHSKAYA LINE

③ ARBATSKO-POKROVSKAYA LINE

④ RING LINE

⑤ KALUZHSKO-RIZHSKAYA LINE

⑥ FILIOVSKAYA LINE

METRO MAP

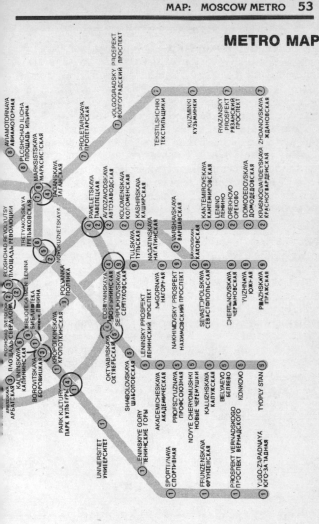

(7) ZHDANOVSKO-KRASNOPRESNENSKAYA LINE

(8) KALININSKAYA LINE

(9) SERPUKHOVSKAYA LINE

STATIONS FOR CHANGING TRAINS

Buses, Trolley-buses and Streetcars. Included in Moscow's extensive system of mass transit are separate routes for some 320 buses, 75 trolley-buses, and 50 street-cars, or trams, known to Russians as *tramvai* . Like the metro, rides cost 5 kopeks (less than a penny) for a ticket, or *taloni*, which can be purchased from the driver.

Tourists planning to use Moscow's network of mass transportation for more than two weeks should purchase monthly or half-monthly passes called *yedini*. A full-month pass covering the metro, trolley-bus, tram and bus systems costs only 6 rubles ($1). Separate passes for each are also available. The buses run from 6 AM to 1 AM and trams from 5:30 AM to 1:30 AM.

Rental Cars. Rental cars with and without chauffeurs are available at some hotels and through the Intourist service bureau on Gorky Street. Renting a car without a driver is not recommended unless you are familiar with Moscow's intricate maze of streets. Traffic keeps to the right. Parking is permitted virtually everywhere except Red Square and the Kremlin. When leaving your car, you will be right in step with the average Muscovite if you remove your windshield wipers — they're hard to replace and are hot items for petty thieves. Parking lights, instead of full headlights, are used while driving at night. Traffic police patrol the streets on foot and bran-dish black-and-white-striped clubs to stop drivers who may be breaking the law.

MONEY MATTERS

Currency. The monetary unit in the Soviet Union is the ruble. The ruble is nonconvertible, and thus is essentially worthless outside the U.S.S.R. One ruble equals 100 ko-peks. Paper money consists of 1-, 2-, 3-, 5-, 10-, 25-, 50- and 100-ruble notes. The coinage consists of 1-, 2-, 3-, 5-, 10-, 15-, 20- and 50-kopek and 1-ruble coins. In April 1990, the official exchange rate for business transactions, including direct investment in joint ventures, was one ruble to $1.67. The tourist exchange rate at that time, on the other hand, was 6.2 rubles to $1.00, while the black market rate ranged from 15 to 20 rubles to $1.00.

Restrictions. Rubles may not be brought into or taken out of the U.S.S.R., except for two rubles that may be taken as souvenirs. It's best to exchange currency in small amounts and only at authorized exchange institutions (Soviet banks or exchange offices). An entry declaration must be presented each time currency is converted, so keep all receipts for these transactions, as well as for individual purchases. If you do not, you may find it impossible to reconvert your unspent rubles back into dollars. It is illegal to accept offers to exchange currency outside of these organizations, and foreigners, including U.S. citizens, have been arrested for exchanging currency on the black market. It is also worth mentioning that a person obtaining rubles on the black market may find no place to spend them, because most charges to foreign visitors (e.g., hotel rooms, auto rentals, airline tickets, overseas telephone calls) must be paid in hard currency. Hence, on arrival at the airport, a foreign businessperson is likely to be offered up to 20 rubles for $1.00; discover at the hotel that the official tourist rate is 6.25 rubles to $1.00; and then later learn that for the purposes of investment in the U.S.S.R., the official Soviet exchange rate is only 60 kopeks to $1.00.

Credit Cards. MasterCard, American Express, Carte Blanche, Diner's Club, Eurocard, and Visa are widely accepted in the major cities of the Soviet Union. An anomaly which has not been corrected as of this writing should be noted by credit card users. If you change U.S. dollars to rubles at an official exchange location (e.g., the cashier at your hotel), you will receive 6.25 rubles for every dollar you exchange. On the other hand, you must pay your hotel bill or your overseas phone bill or the fee for your hotel car with your credit card, and you will be charged at the far less favorable exchange rate of 1 U.S. dollar equal to 65 kopeks. Hence, if your hotel bill is 100 rubles, the charge to you will be about $140, that is, the rate of about one ruble equals $1.40. Were you able to pay for your 100-ruble hotel room in rubles obtained from a lawful exchange, it would cost you only about $16.00. If you could pay for the room with black market rubles obtained at the 20:1 rate, that same room would cost you $5.00. Such are the vicissitudes of foreign exchange.

Traveler's Checks. American Express, Bank of America, Barclays Bank, Citibank, Deak Perera, Perera

Express, the Republic National Bank of Dallas and Thomas Cook traveler's checks are readily accepted in most Soviet cities.

Tipping. Notwithstanding what has previously been said about resisting the demands of taxi drivers, among others, for foreign goods instead of rubles in payment of fares, a business visitor will often meet a situation in which he will want to express appreciation, or request a small favor. A tip of a ruble or two may often suffice in these circumstances, but chances are that a far more appreciated gift would be a package of foreign cigarettes, a disposable cigarette lighter, a ballpoint pen, a cassette tape of Western music, an inexpensive pocket calculator, a key chain or a nail clipper.

COMMUNICATIONS

Telephone. Telephone directories as they are known in the rest of the developed world are not available in Moscow. Thus, you are well advised, to the extent possible, to obtain all necessary business and personal Moscow telephone numbers before leaving the U.S. Lack of telephone number information makes business cards valuable. Hold onto the business cards given to you by Soviet officials. Check at once to see if the card you receive contains a telephone number; if not, be sure to ask for one.

There are usually no central hotel switchboards, so after you have registered at your hotel, you must find out your hotel room telephone number and give it to your contacts in the U.S.S.R. and those at home. This number is usually written on the telephone itself, or appears in a phone number list found inside the booklet of information on your writing table. That same list may show the phone number of every other room in the hotel, by room number, so if you are traveling with others who are staying at the same hotel, knowing their room numbers is the key to getting their telephone numbers.

In nearly every case, your hotel room telephone number is a direct-dial outside line. This means that you can dial outside local calls directly from your hotel room, although it should be noted that from some of these phones you must dial a prefix of "0" or "9." The disadvantage to hotel phone systems is that if you are not in your room to receive an incoming call, it will go unanswered; there is usually no hotel switchboard that takes calls or messages for you. You may book outgoing overseas telephone calls either through the *dezhurnaya* on your floor, or at the hotel reception desk in the lobby.

Direct-dial long distance telephone service is available at the U.S. Commerce Office, although that office understandably cannot function as a telephone service for all business visitors. For their clients, the service firms (e.g., the Moscow offices of the U.S. law firms and accounting firms referred to later in this booklet) commonly offer a direct-dial overseas telephone service.

For local calls from public telephones in Moscow, carry several 2-kopek coins. Because these are the only coins that public telephones will accept, they are often (and quite predictably) very difficult to come by. In Moscow and Leningrad, you deposit the coin before picking up the receiver and dialing.

A word of warning: the Moscow telephone system leaves a lot to be desired. It is often difficult to get a dial tone when you pick up the telephone receiver to make a call. After you finally do get a dial tone, you're frequently interrupted by a busy signal after dialing one or two numbers. Then you must begin the process again. As if that isn't enough, phones often go unanswered in the Soviet Union. If your call is answered, but the person you want to speak to isn't available, the answerer will in all likelihood hang up abruptly — without taking a message. To avoid this, have a Russian-speaking person place your calls if possible.

Telecommunications. These services are available to and from the Soviet Union; you will probably be able to communicate from the U.S. with your business contacts in the U.S.S.R. by telex or fax. For access to telex and telecopy services for outgoing messages while you are inMoscow, contact the service desk in your hotel, or the law firm, consultant, bank or accounting firm which acts for you in Moscow.

Postal Services. The U.S. government has signed an international pact with the Soviet Union that allows the exchange of expedited mail shipments between the two countries. As a result of this agreement, customers are able to get improved delivery service from the U.S. to Moscow through Express Mail International Service (EMS). Nevertheless, business correspondence — like all other correspondence — between the Soviet Union and the rest of the world is slow and unpredictable. Nor are things much better within the Soviet Union. Many businesses in Moscow use staff messengers to deliver letters and packages.

EMS mail to Moscow from the U.S. will be delivered the same day, Monday through Friday, if it arrives in Moscow before 5:00 AM. On Saturdays, Sundays and national holidays, delivery will be made only if the addressee's office is open. Further information can be obtained by calling the U.S. Postal Service at (202) 682-9595.

Hotels offer limited postal services, where you can buy stamps and mail letters and small packages. You should not wrap packages beforehand: The post office sells boxes and insists that the wrapping be done there. You will also have to fill out numerous forms with each package.

Courier Services. Because international postage service between the Soviet Union and the rest of the world is so slow, business letters, packages and documents are normally sent by private courier. Both Federal Express and DHL Worldwide Express offer small parcel air courier services between the U.S. and U.S.S.R. These services have proven nearly indispensible to U.S. firms that must exchange documentation with business partners in the U.S.S.R. Soviet postal service is notoriously poor, and, though available, telecopy facilities are sometimes uncertain and nearly always unsuitable for the transmission of lengthy documents.

TIPS FOR THE MOSCOW VISITOR

Tips for the Business Visitor

Obtaining Business Services in Moscow. After arriving in Moscow, you may discover that you need such services as assistance with typing, photocopying, sending or receiving telexes and telecopies, translation, interpretation, guides or drivers. The service desk in your hotel may be able to direct you to a business service department within the hotel. But the availability (or reliability) of such services cannot be counted on.

As noted on page 104, the U.S. Commercial Office offers some business services. If you or your firm is a member of the U.S.-U.S.S.R. Trade and Economic Council, you may be able to obtain assistance at the Council's Moscow office. If you have a relationship with a foreign law firm, bank, accounting firm or consulting service that maintains a Moscow office, you can turn to them for business service assistance.

If you expect that you will need photocopying machines while in Moscow, you should be aware that copiers are not readily available at the offices of many Soviet enterprises or at government offices. If possible, bulk copying should be handled before your arrival in the U.S.S.R.

Business Cards. It is a good idea to bring a sufficient number of your business cards in English, and in Russian too, if possible. Telephone books are not readily available and the exchange of cards between Soviet officials and foreign visitors has become an indispensable tool for future communication.

Business Gifts. Business visitors may wish to leave small souvenirs with Soviet business contacts and other people, such as hotel employees and hired drivers. When choosing gifts to bring to the U.S.S.R. bear in mind that Soviet customs officers may charge you hefty ad valorem duty on gifts. For that reason, among others, small gifts of nominal value may be best. Your prospective business partner may be most pleased to have a gift that relates in some way to your company or your industry. Soviets are especially fond of lapel pins commemorating events, places, companies, products or the like. In the event that a Soviet official should hint or ask that a gift of some valuable item, or cash, should be made, you would be well advised to explain that the U.S. has a law, the Foreign Corrupt Practices Act, which can impose criminal penalties on U.S. business representatives who make gifts to officials of a foreign state under certain circumstances.

Business Hours and Public Holidays. Business hours in Moscow are from 9 AM to 5 PM, with lunch taken between 12 noon and 2 PM. Business luncheons generally start at about 1 PM and linger until 3 PM or beyond. A disproportionate number of Muscovites (especially housewives) take time away from their jobs at mid-day not to eat lunch, but to take care of such domestic chores as waiting in long lines for scarce food items. This custom, however, is not usually practiced by the officials who are likely to meet with foreign business visitors.

The official public holidays of the Soviet Union — those days on which government offices, shops and other businesses are closed — are:

January 1	New Year's Day
February 23	Soviet Army Day
March 8	International Women's Day
May 1–2	May Day (International Labor Day)
May 9	Victory Day (1945)
October 7	Constitution Day
November 7–8	Anniversary of the Great October Socialist Revolution (1917)

Tips for the General Visitor

Time. The U.S.S.R, with its enormous breadth, occupies 11 of the world's 24 time zones. Moscow is Greenwich Mean Time *plus* 3 hours; Moscow is thus 8 hours ahead of U.S. Eastern Time (both Standard and Daylight Times, although Moscow returns to Standard Time from Daylight Time a bit earlier in the fall than the U.S.). To be sure, check with your long-distance phone company.

The country's 11 time zones work as follows: when it is noon Eastern Standard Time in the U.S., it is 8 PM in Moscow; 9 PM in Volgograd; 10 PM in Sverdlovsk; 11 PM in Omsk; 12 midnight in Krasnoyarsk; 1 AM in Irkutsk; 2 AM in Chita; 3 AM in Vladivostok; 4 AM in Magadan; 5 AM in Petropavlovsk; and 6 AM in Anadyr.

Electricity. Guaranteed to get your hackles up, so come prepared. Electric current varies from 110 to

127 to 220 volts AC, 50 cycles.

To avert disaster, all electric appliances made for use in the U.S. (e.g., electric razors, hair dryers, battery rechargers and copiers) must be operated with converters and transformers, neither of which are generally available in the U.S.S.R. Convenient, all-purpose converter kits can be purchased in the U.S.

Weights and Measures. The Soviet Union uses the metric system. Hence, unless it is a significant inconvenience to you, your business correspondence with Soviet parties, including business proposals and draft contract documents, should use the metric system. For your convenience, a conversion chart is contained in the Appendix of this book.

Personal Safety. Petty street crime is on the increase in Moscow. Exercise prudence at all times. Don't travel after dark, except in groups. Don't make an ostentatious display of anything of value (e.g., your passport, credit cards, watches, rings, jewelry, cameras, currency or such items as portable telephones or laptop computers). Don't invite strangers to your room. Many business visitors who must be out late at night for banquets or business meetings arrange to be transported by a car and driver reserved through their hotel. This is done because there have been instances of foreigners being attacked while vainly trying to hail taxis late at night and, though rare, of robberies perpetrated by gypsy cabdrivers.

Photography. While foreigners have been arrested and expelled from the Soviet Union for photographing prohibited subjects, chances are that it is permissible to photograph most of what you will be interested in. If you are on a business visit to a manufacturing plant or other such facility, you should always ask your host before you take photographs. Permission is normally granted, but keep in mind that there may be many reasons why you cannot photograph a plant. In addition, exercise common sense when taking pictures while sightseeing. It is perfectly permissible to photograph points of historic interest, but do not thrust your camera into the faces of people in Moscow any more than you would do so at home. Keep in mind that you will very likely find it difficult to buy film for your camera in Moscow. If it is available, it will be considerably more expensive than it is at home. Bring a supply of your own.

Access to News. Unless you are staying at the Savoy or the Mezhdunarodnaya, where Cable News Network telecasts are available on the television in your room 24 hours a day, and where *USA Today* (but no other Western newspaper or periodical) is sold in the lobby, you will be essentially cut off from news of the outside world. For this reason, many experienced business travelers carry a small short-wave radio. Reception from Voice of America and the British Broadcasting Corporation is good, because the Soviets no longer interfere with these broadcasts. If you read Russian, you will find some coverage of world news in *Pravda* and *Izvestia*, the Party and State newspapers, respectively. *Moscow News*, available in several foreign languages including English, carries interesting coverage of Soviet politics and economics.

MAJOR TOURIST ATTRACTIONS

There is so much to see and do in Moscow that even the most durable tourists find sightseeing exhausting. A good introduction is the three- to four-hour Intourist city tour by doubledecker bus, for which you can sign up in your hotel. As an alternative, we'd also advise you to hire a cab for the day; the going rate is 10 to 15 rubles an hour (about $1.65 to $2.50). Below, we will direct you to Moscow's most important and notable sights.

The Kremlin
Your first sightseeing stop should be in the very heart of the city at the Kremlin—the house of government and the nucleus from which the city developed over the centuries in a series of concentric rings. In front of the northwestern entrance to the Kremlin, which served as the city's original fortress, is the **Alexandrovsky Garden.** Here you can see the arresting **grave of the Unknown Soldier,** dedicated on May 9, 1967, the 22nd anniversary of the World War II victory over Nazi Germany. The body under the red granite is that of an unidentified Soviet soldier who died during the autumn of 1941 in the Nazi attack on the village of Kryukovo, outside Moscow.

Directly above you, rising behind the Kremlin facade, you will see a large yellow building known as **the Arsenal.** It was begun by Peter the Great as a museum and military storage site and remodeled at the beginning of the last century. Today, it houses government offices.

The **Armory,** a museum of the Czars' ambassadorial gifts, arms and regalia, stands next to the Arsenal. A rare collection of 17th-century silver, royal carriages and Fabergé eggs highlights this museum, which can only be viewed on an Intourist-guided tour.

One of the most breathtaking sights inside the Kremlin wall is the **Square of the Cathedrals.** Three gold-domed cathedrals, the **Ivan the Great Bell Tower** and the **Granovitaya Palace** frame the Square. Just as dramatic are the cathedrals' colorful interiors, decorated with brilliant frescoes and icons painted by Russian masters. The **Cathedral of the Archangel** houses the tombs of 46 czars and princes. Their likenesses are painted on the walls above each of the tombs.

Bordering the Square, next to the Bell Tower, you will see the cracked **Tsar Bell,** the largest bell in the world. Completed in 1735, it weighs more than 200 tons, and is 20 feet high and 22 feet is diameter. Nearby is the 40-ton **Tsar Cannon.** With a 35-inch bore and a 6-inch-thick barrel, it has the largest caliber of any gun in the world. The most modern building in the Kremlin is the glass and aluminum **Palace of Congresses,** completed in 1967 to house the Soviet Parliament and party congresses.

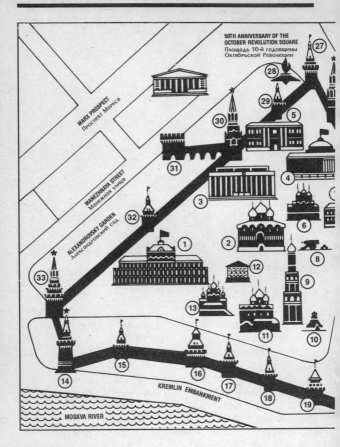

Red Square

Neighboring the Kremlin is one of Moscow's most famous trademarks, **Red Square,** a mile-and-a-half-long rectangle dating back to the 15th century. It was called red (*krasnaya*), which can also mean "beautiful" in Russian, long before the communists came to power in 1917.

The spotlight attraction of Red Square is the **Lenin Mausoleum,** containing the embalmed body of the Soviet Union's ideological and political founder, who died in 1924. It is open on Tuesdays, Wednesdays, Thursdays and Saturdays from 10 AM to 1 PM, and on Sundays from 10 AM to 2 PM. Admission is free, but Intourist passes are required and are available at hotel service bureaus. Lines form next to the red-bricked **State History**

THE KREMLIN

1 Grand Kremlin Palace
2 Cathedral of the Assumption
3 Kremlin Palace of Congress
4 Council of Ministers Building
5 Arsenal
6 Cathedral of the Twelve Apostles
7 Presidium of the Supreme Soviet
   of the U.S.S.R.
8 Tsar Cannon
9 Ivan the Great Bell Tower
10 Tsar Bell
11 Cathedral of the Archangel
12 Granovitaya Palace
13 Cathedral of the
   Annunciation
14 Vodovzvodnaya Tower
15 Annunciation Tower
16 Tainitskaya Tower
17 1st Nameless Tower
18 2nd Nameless Tower
19 Peter Tower
20 Beklemishevskaya Tower
21 Tower of Sts. Constantine
   and Helen
22 Little Czar Tower
23 Spassky Tower
24 Lenin Mausoleum
25 Senate Tower
26 Nikolokaya Tower
27 Corner Arsenal
   (Sobakina) Tower
28 Tomb of the
   Unknown Soldier
29 Middle Arsenal Tower
30 Troitskaya Tower
31 Kutafya Tower
32 Armory Tower
33 Borovitskaya Tower
34 St. Basil's Cathedral
35 Monument to Kuzma Minin
   and Dmitry Pozharsky
36 State History Museum

Museum, which flanks Red Square. Cameras are not allowed inside the mausoleum. The authenticity of Lenin's remains is sometimes questioned by foreign visitors, but the Soviet government maintains they are genuine and recently closed the mausoleum for various renovations.

Behind the Lenin mausoleum, in the Kremlin wall, are the tombs of other Soviet leaders, including Leonid Brezhnev, Yuri Andropov, Konstantin Chernenko and Josef Stalin (he once rested next to Lenin in the mausoleum). The Square is also enclosed by the G.U.M. department store and the stunning 16th-century St. **Basil's Cathedral,** which is well-known throughout the world for its colorful, swirling onion domes.

25TH OCTOBER STREET
УЛИЦА
25-ГО
ОКТЯБРЯ

Lenin Hills

On a clear day, visit Lenin Hills, where you may enjoy a spectacular view of the city and the towering edifice of **Moscow State University.** As you overlook the city from there, you will see the sparkling gold domes of the **Novodevichy Cemetery and Convent,** which should be your next stop. Once used by noble women, the Convent is enclosed by a crenelated wall and 12 battle towers. Evdokia, Peter the Great's first wife, and Princess Sophia, his conniving sister, were both banished here by Peter.

The **Cemetary** is the second most prestigious burial ground in the Soviet Union, after the Kremlin. Khrushchev, Gromyko, Chekhov, Gogol and Bulgakov rest here

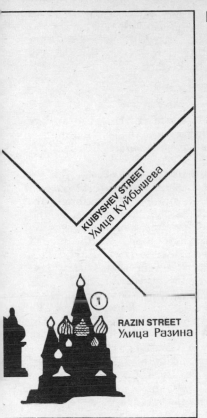

RED SQUARE

1   St. Basil's Cathedral
    (Cathedral of
    the Intercession)
2   Monument to Kuzma Minin
    and Dmitry Pozharsky
3   Spassky Tower
4   Lenin Mausoleum
5   Presidium of the Supreme
    Soviet of the U.S.S.R.
6   Council of Ministers Building
7   Senate Tower
8   Nikolskaya Tower
9   State History Museum

among eminent artists, scientists and military and political leaders.

Westerners are often impressed by the gigantic permanent **Exhibition of Economic Achievements,** known as VDNKh (*vuh-juh-enn-KHAH*). This 553-acre monument, across from the Cosmos Hotel, includes about 80 ornate pavilions that show off and, in some cases, exaggerate the country's scientific and economic progress.

Spend the rest of your sightseeing tour exploring a few of Moscow's 150 museums and galleries and 100 parks, including famous **Gorky Park.** Museums' hours vary widely. Many are frequently under renovation. Even Red Square and the Kremlin are closed on short notice for unannounced reasons. Check schedules with your hotel service bureau before all your excursions. Most museums and sights charge a small entrance fee, which is payable in rubles. Here is a short list of some of the other sightseeing highlights:

Museums

Andrei Rublyev Museum, in the Andronikov Monastery, 10 Pryamikov Square. This museum is devoted to one of Russia's most celebrated icon painters.

Museum of the Revolution, 21 Gorky Street. Opened in 1926, this 37-room museum displays artifacts and memorabilia from the Revolution. Many exhibits are pure Soviet progaganda that hyperbolizes Josef Stalin's contribution to the 1917 Revolution and diminishes the roles of others. Before the Revolution, it was the English Club for noblemen. Open 10 AM to 6 PM Tuesday, Saturday and Sunday; noon to 8 PM Wednesday; 11 AM to 7 PM Friday. Closed Monday and Thursday.

Pushkin Fine Arts Gallery, 12 Volkhonka Street. The largest museum in the country, after the Hermitage in Leningrad. Completed in 1912 (when it was known as Alexander III's Museum), it contains a fine collection of ancient Egyptian art and paintings by Botticelli, Rembrandt, Rubens, Van Dyck, Constable, Poussin, Watteau, Cézanne, Gauguin and Matisse (be mindful, however, that many of the museum's pieces are reproductions). Open from 10 AM to 8 PM Tuesday through Saturday and from 10 AM to 6 PM on Sundays. Closed Mondays.

State History Museum, 1-2 Red Square. This museum covers Russian history from its beginnings to the end of the 19th century. Completed in 1883, it was the original site of Moscow University. With 300,000 exhibits, the museum houses the country's largest collection of historical materials, including coins, medals, ancient manuscripts and even the bed Napoleon left behind when he fled Russia. Open Monday, Thursday, Saturday and Sunday, 10 AM to 6 PM; Wednesday and Friday 11 AM to 7 PM. Closed Tuesday and on the last Monday of each month.

Train of Mourning, at Paveletsky Railway Station, 1 Kozhenichesky Square. This is the engine and carriage that brought the coffin with Lenin's body to Moscow. It is more interesting that it sounds, especially if you enjoy looking at antique trains.

Tretyakov Art Galley, 10 Lavrushinsky Pereulok. Moscow's finest art gallery, focusing on the history of Russian art. The original collection was donated by the brothers Pavel and Sergei Tretyakov in 1856. It contains more than 5,000 paintings, 3,000 works of ancient Russian art, about 900 sculptures and 30,000 drawings and engravings. The gallery is located next to its own metro station. Open every day except Mondays from 10 AM to 8 PM. Latest admission is 7 PM.

SHOPPING

Shopping in Moscow is more of a cultural and educational eye-opener than a treasure hunt. But contrary to popular belief, it is possible to buy attractive things in Moscow. It just takes patience and perseverance.

There are no comparable Soviet versions of such Western stores as Bloomingdale's, Saks Fifth Avenue or Macy's, although Estée Lauder and Christian Dior recently opened shops in Moscow. One of the best places to shop is the historic, pedestrian-only section of Moscow known as the Arbat. Here you will find a plethora of shops and street vendors along pricey Arbat Street, the city's intellectual vortex. Beautiful hand-crafted *matryoshka* dolls and lacquer boxes sell for the equivalent of hundreds of dollars. Rare books and antique samovars are also sold. On the street, artists work and exhibit their creations, much of which are acerbic commentary on Soviet life and politics.

On weekends from dawn to dusk, do not miss the new outdoor flea market, called *vernisage,* at Ismailovo Park. This year-round spectacle, which began in the summer of 1989, offers some of the best bargains in town on the country's finest *matryoshkas,* lacquer boxes, icons and antiques (all payments must be in rubles). Here you also will see Soviet democracy and *glasnost* at their peak. Bold merchants display pins, works of art, banners, dolls and various knickknacks that deride the Soviet Government and its more infamous leaders. Leonid Brezhnev and Josef Stalin are the two most ridiculed figures, often caricatured in the form of piggy banks, *matryoshka* dolls and other figurines. Even Lenin and Gorbachev do not escape humiliating depictions.

Prices at Ismailovo are usually determined spontaneously and arbitrarily. Westerners are easily identifiable there and are expected to pay more than Soviets. Do not buy anything without bargaining, and try to find a Soviet to represent you in the negotiations. Some merchants will personally design political and apolitical *matryoshka* dolls for you. It is illegal to pay for anything in foreign currency (the authorities strictly patrol the area).

It is difficult to rate Moscow's shops, because their merchandise changes almost daily. Due to drastic shortages, Soviet shoppers tend to hoard items as soon as they arrive in the stores. This is not true in the well-stocked *beryozkas,* which only accept foreign currency. Most stores are open Monday through Saturday from 8 AM to 9 PM, except for a one-hour lunch break, usually from 1 to 2 or 2 to 3. The main shopping streets are Gorky, Arbat, Kuznetsky Most and Kalinin Prospect.

What There Is to Buy

The best known of Russian souvenirs are the sets of dolls called *matryoshka.* These brightly colored dolls sometimes contain more than a dozen different-sized figurines, one inside the other. Also popular with Westerners are the miniature lacquer pieces designed by artisans of Soviet villages like Palekh, Mstyora, and Fedoskino. The miniatures include tiny pill boxes, brooches, and elegant jewelry boxes, with hand-painted scenes and characters from Russian fairy tales and biblical events.

Where to Buy

Beryozkas (foreign-currency stores). If you are on a short business trip or on a quick tour, the most expedient way to shop is at the *beryozkas*, which are located in all Intourist hotels. These stores, which do not accept rubles, carry imported groceries, handcrafted lacquerware, furs, amber jewelry, books, electronics and many other items.

Compared to Soviet stores that accept rubles, *beryozkas* offer more variety and better-quality goods, albeit at much higher prices. They are also less crowded (Soviets are not allowed to shop in them) and more convenient. Ascertaining actual prices at *beryozkas,* however, can be tricky. First, all items are listed in rubles, even though they must be purchased in foreign currency. Second, the exchange rate at *beryozkas* is different from the official rate at which tourists convert their money into rubles. At a *beryozka,* one ruble equals about $1.60, while at banks and exchange offices, one ruble is exchanged for only about 16 cents.

Another caveat: unless you are planning a trip around the world, bring small bills and coins to the *beryozka;* change comes in bizarre (and often unspendable) combinations of foreign currency. You may pay in cash, traveler's checks or credit cards. The largest and best *beryozkas* are at the Rossiya, Ukraina and Mezhdunarodnaya hotels. The two-floor *beryozka* across from Novodevichy Cemetery has an excellent selection of Russian vodka, fur hats and electronics.

Shops Accepting Soviet Rubles. If you have time for leisurely shopping and are up to the adventure, explore some Soviet stores. Although self-service shops are only now beginning to appear in Moscow, you will find that buying anything in most Soviet stores can be an incredible hassle. To purchase items, you must first approach the counter where they are located and find out their prices. Then, you must pay a cashier and obtain a receipt that lists the price of the items you are buying. Finally, you must return to the first counter and show your receipt to collect the desired items. In crowded shops, this can mean standing in long lines three times over.

You may find bargains at second-hand stores, known as **commission shops** (*kommisioniye magazini*). These stores specialize in a wide variety of jewelry, antiques, furnishings and arts and crafts. People bring their personal items here and the shop receives a commission for selling them (hence the name).

Also visit one of Moscow's farmers' markets, known as *rynoks* (the Tsentralnyi Rynok, on 15 Tsvetnoi Boulevard, is the biggest). Here you will find a colorful smorgasbord of fresh fruit, vegetables, herbs and flowers. Animated merchants sell their home-grown produce at high prices, but expect you to bargain with them. One of the most interesting is the **Pet Market** (Ptichy Rynok), held on weekends at 42 Kalitnikovskaya Street, southeast of Taganka Square.

Following is a list of some of the best stores that accept rubles.

Detskyi Mir ("Children's World"), 2 Marx Prospect. A huge department store specializing in children's goods. Brace yourself for crowds. Open every day from 8 AM to 9 PM

Dom Knigi ("House of the Book"), 26 Kalinin Prospect. The largest bookshop in Moscow. Sometimes sells books in English.

G.U.M. State Universal Department Store, 3 Red Square. Everything about this airy building is impressive, except its contents. Erected in the 19th century as a department store, it sells items ranging from ties to perfume to ice cream. Westerners joke about how difficult it is to find something of quality here. Open Monday through Friday, from 11 AM to 9 PM, and Saturday from 8 AM to 9 PM.

Khristal, 15 Gorky Street. Sells jewelry, vases, wine glasses and lacquer boxes, but the selection is limited.

Melodiya, next to Dom Knigi on Kalinin Street, sells records and sheet music.

Progress Bookstore, Zubovsky Boulevard across from the headquarters of the Novosti Press Agency, near the Park Kultury metro station. Specializes in books in foreign languages, but precious few that you'd actually want to read.

Russkyi Souvenir, 9 Kutuzovsky Prospect. One of the best selections of lacquer boxes, ceramics and *matryoshkas.* Open Monday through Saturday from 11 AM to 8 PM.

Stamp Collectors' Shop, 16 Dzerzhinsky Street.

T.S.U.M. Central Department Store, 2 Petrovka Street. A mall of 12 shops, this is a modern version of G.U.M. in a less attractive building. Open Monday through Friday from 11 AM to 9 PM; Saturday from 8 AM to 9 PM.

CULTURE, ENTERTAINMENT
AND NIGHTLIFE

An evening out in Moscow can result in culture shock. There is no such thing as impromptu bar hopping or restaurant shopping. Spontaneity is unheard of — almost every nocturnal activity requires reservations that are often difficult to obtain. For those who do not speak Russian, the nightlife choices are limited: you can attend operas, ballets, concerts, sporting events, circuses or restaurants with musical entertainment and dancing.

Ballet and Opera

Moscow offers some of the finest ballet and opera in the world. Tickets to both can be purchased only in foreign currency at your hotel or at the Intourist service bureau on Gorky Street. Tickets to the Bolshoi Opera and Ballet Theater cost many times the actual ruble price written on the ticket. Few besides the privileged Soviet elite can find or buy these tickets for rubles. Black marketeers almost always scalp the tickets for foreign currency outside the Bolshoi Theater. Evening performances at all theaters begin at 7 PM, and weekend matinees begin at noon. Check the schedules at the service bureau in your hotel.

Bolshoi Opera and Ballet Theater. Sverdlov Square (tel.: 292-9986). Once you step into the crimson and gold interior of this stately building, you feel as if you have exited the U.S.S.R. and returned to the imperial Russia of the czars. Or you may imagine you are back in the West, because Americans and Europeans pack this theater. Formerly known as the Great Imperial Theater, it was completely rebuilt after a fire in 1854. The Bolshoi (the word means "big") now seats 2,155 people. Even though some of its stars have defected, the performers who have remained are impressive. Its repertory includes traditional and often stodgy renditions of classical ballets and operas. In performance terms, *The Nutcracker*, *Swan Lake* and *Giselle* are by far the better ballets. *Boris Godunov* and *Eugene Onegin* are the better operas. Tickets to the Bolshoi are officially priced in rubles, but can only be purchased from Intourist or your hotel for foreign currency of much higher value. If you are late for a performance, you will be barred from entering the auditorium until the intermission. Soviet champagne, coffee, soda, caviar, sandwiches and candy are sold in the lobby before performances and during intermission, but you can expect absurdly long lines. Inexpensive classical music albums are sold in the large waiting halls on the floor above the lobby. The Bolshoi occasionally performs in the Kremlin at the 6,000-seat Palace of Congresses, the home of the Soviet Parliament.

Stanislavsky and Nemirovich-Danchenko Musical Theater, 17 Pushkin Street (tel.: 271-2826). An underrated opera and ballet house in the shadow of the more established Bolshoi Theater. Many Soviets prefer the Stanislavsky to the Bolshoi for its modern operas and ballets.

Drama
Moscow's drama theaters are superb, but difficult to enjoy without a knowledge of Russian. The works of such playwrights as Shakespeare, Molière, Chekhov, Ibsen, Pushkin, Tennessee Williams and Arthur Miller are regularly performed at many of Moscow's theaters, and are worth seeing for their staging and acting. Tickets can be purchased in foreign currency at Intourist or at your hotel service bureau. Tickets to less popular performances are sold for rubles at theater box offices or at kiosks in the downtown area.

Lenin Komsomol Theater, 6 Chekhov Street (tel.: 299-9668). Known simply as the Len-Kom, this is the hottest theater in Moscow. With its dynamic staging and acting, this is Moscow's "Midas" theater, turning unknown plays into masterpieces.

Moscow Art Theater (MKHAT), 22 Tverskoy Boulevard (tel.: 203-6222). This is the mother of all theaters in the Soviet Union. Founded in 1898 by Konstantin Stanislavsky (the father of "method" acting) and Vladimir Nemirovich-Danchenko, MKHAT (em-KHOTT) is known for its traditional productions of Russian classics by Chekhov, Ostrovsky and others. Its new building seats 1,360 and includes facilities for simultaneous translation into four languages.

Obraztsov Puppet Theater, 3 Sadovaya-Samotechnaya Street (tel.: 299-6313). Here you will find entertaining puppet shows for both children and adults, plus a remarkable museum featuring hand-made puppets from around the world. *Don Juan* is a perennial favorite.

Taganka Drama and Comedy Theater, 76 Chkalova Street (tel.: 271-2826). The most famous theater in Moscow, once led by the well-known Soviet director Yuri Lubimov. Productions are innovative and polished, but many say the Taganka lost its edge after its leading actor, Vladimir Vyssotsky, died unexpectedly in 1980. Especially recommended are its productions of *Ten Days That Shook the World, The Cherry Orchard* and *The Master and Margarita.*

Concert Halls
Music is to Moscow what drama is to London. Scores of concert halls regularly feature some of the world's best symphony orchestras, soloists and song and dance ensembles. Tickets can be purchased in rubles at the concert hall.

Conservatory, 13 Herzen Street (tel.: 299-7412). One of the world's greatest concert halls. Leading musicians from the U.S.S.R. and abroad perform in this elegant Baroque auditorium. Since 1958, it has hosted the International Tchaikovsky Competition for violinists, cellists and vocalists.

Tchaikovsky Concert Hall, Mayakovsky Square (tel.: 299-3487). Another landmark of classical and folk music, with excellent acoustics. Try to see a *beryozka* (not to be confused with the foreign-currency stores of the same name), which is an ensemble of folk dances from different regions of the U.S.S.R.

Circus
The circus is a favorite outing for many tourists. But expect to be disappointed if you have already seen the Moscow Circus perform outside the Soviet Union. The most talented circus stars rarely perform in their homeland. The one-ring shows, nevertheless, are often amusing and entertaining. Many acrobatic stunts will impress and surprise you. The **Old Circus,** housed on 13 Tsvetnoy Boulevard in a handsome building that was

recently renovated by a Finnish company, offers the best show in town. Further away from the city center, near Moscow State University, the **New Circus** on 7 Vernadsky Prospect is less polished, but entertaining. Tickets can be purchased at highly inflated foreign currency prices at the Intourist and hotel service bureaus, or sometimes at the circus box offices up until show time.

Sporting Events
Soccer, hockey and basketball are the most popular spectator sports in the U.S.S.R. Games are played in various arenas around the city. Check the sports schedule at your hotel, and buy your tickets, which are inexpensive, in rubles at kiosks in the downtown area.

RELIGIOUS SERVICES

Moscow has over 400 churches, but not all of them are open for services. Most services begin at 7 AM and 10 AM on Sundays and holy days, and 8 AM and 6 PM on weekdays. Appropriate attire is required—women must wear skirts or dresses for Russian Orthodox services and scarves or other head coverings at Old Believers' services. Men should wear hats or yarmulkas at synagogue services. Do not put your hands in your pockets—it is considered disrespectful.

Anglican and **Protestant** church services are held on alternate Sundays at Spaso House (the U.S. ambassador's residence) and at the British Embassy (14 Maurice Thorez Embankment, tel.: 231-8511) at 10:30 AM (10 AM in the summer); Sunday school is held at the same time and place as the church services.

Baptist services are held on Sundays at 10 AM, 2 and 6 PM, and on Thursdays at 6 PM. The church address is 3 Maly Vuzovsky Pereulok, tel.: 297-5167.

Roman Catholic services are held at St. Louis des Français, 12 Malaya Lubyanka, on Sundays at 8 and 11 AM and at 6 PM on Saturdays. Masses are in Latin, sermons in Russian and Polish. Sunday masses are also held at the U.S. Commercial Office, next to the American Embassy, 19/23 Tchaikovsky Street, at 10 AM in English and at noon in French.

Theroux

Old Believers' services are held at the Cathedral on 29 Rogozhsky Pereulok (tel.: 361-5193), and at many other churches around the city.

Russian Orthodox services are held at more than 40 churches, including the Uspenskaya ("Assumption," or "Dormition") Church, at 2 Bolshaya Pirogovskaya Street, in the Novodevichy Convent. Most of these services begin at 8 AM and 6 PM on weekdays and at 7 AM and 10 AM on Sundays and holy days.

Moscow has two **Jewish synagogues** that conduct services one hour before sundown on Fridays and at 10 AM on Saturdays. They are located at 8 Arkhipova Street and at 8 Bolshoi Spasoglinishchevsky Pereulok.

Moscow's only **mosque** is located at 7 Vypolzov Pereulok. The Hamaz is recited five times daily and on Fridays at 1 PM.

HEALTH AND FITNESS

Health Care. If you become ill during your visit and have to be hospitalized, you may find that your hospital stay is somewhat prolonged. Medical care is usually competent, but some visitors have found that Soviet doctors are reluctant to release them from the hospital if the cause of the illness has not been pinpointed, even when the symptoms have apparently disappeared. Should you have to be hospitalized, notify the American Embassy at once.

The U.S. Public Health Service has warned that many U.S. visitors to the U.S.S.R., particularly to Leningrad, have returned to the U.S. infected with the intestinal parasite *Giardia lamblia*. This infection is probably contracted by drinking tap water. To avoid contracting this parasite, travelers should drink only bottled carbonated water, beverages that have been boiled, bottled carbonated soft drinks, beer or wine. Ice cubes in drinks should be avoided. Bottled water should be used for brushing teeth. Salads, fruits that cannot be peeled, and uncooked vegetables should be avoided. Travelers may want to carry iodine tablets to disinfect drinking water. Visitors to the Soviet Union who return with a diarrheal illness lasting more than five days should consult a physician and have a stool specimen examined for parasites.

Visitors intending to stay in the Soviet Union for a period longer than three months may be subject to a medical examination for the detection of Acquired Immune Deficiency Syndrome (AIDS). Persons refusing the examination, or found to be carrying the AIDS virus, may be expelled from the U.S.S.R.

The travel advisory for the area of Kiev issued by the U.S. Department of State following the April 1986 accident at the Chernobyl nuclear power station has been cancelled, and in the view of U.S. authorities levels of radiation are no longer of any known significance to the traveler.

Jogging and Fitness. Joggers—mostly business visitors from the West — are now a fairly common sight in Moscow, especially in the vicinity of the large hotels. A favorite circuit for guests at the Rossiya, National, Intourist, Moscow and Savoy hotels is around (or through) Red Square or the 2-km (1¼-mi) run around the perimeter of the Kremlin. Fitness and exercise facilities in Moscow hotels are still limited, so early morning runs, walks or jogs are the principal means of keeping fit during short stays. Foul winter weather does interfere with a daily jogging regimen, though the main thoroughfares are kept reasonably clear of snow.

MOSCOW TOURISM DIRECTORY

Health and Emergency Services

Emergency medical aid (at hotel)	298-5710
24-hour emergency first aid or ambulance (no coin needed in pay phone)	03
American Embassy doctor (medical and dental)	252-2451
Fire	01
Militia	02

24-hour pharmacies

19-21 October 25 Street	924-6451
	221-4942
74 Leningrad Prospect	151-9764
10 Smolenskaya Square	241-9882

Clinics

Clinic, 12 Herzen Street	229-7323
Intourist Clinic, 2 Gruzinsky Prospect	254-4396
Diplomatic Polyclinic, 4 Dobryninsky Pereulok	237-5933

Travel Services

Intourist Information (in Russian, English, German, and French, 9AM–9PM)   203-6962

Airlines

Sheremetyevo Airport	
Information	155-0922
Intourist (at Sheremetyevo I)	578-5975/69
Intourist (at Sheremetyevo II)	578-5633/14
Aeroflot	
Departures and arrivals	155-0922
Departures and arrivals (in Russian English, German, and French)	245-0002
Air France	237-2325/3344/6777
Alitalia	923-9840/56
British Airways	253-2492
Finnair	292-8788/3337
KLM	253-2150 – 53/2230

Lufthansa	921-9293
	923-0576
Pan Am	253-2658/59
Sabena	248-1214
	230-2241
Swissair	253-8988/1859–60

Rail

Byelorussky Railroad Station	253-4908
Kazansky Railroad Station	266-2542
Kievsky Railroad Station	240-7622
Kursky Railroad Station	266-5652
Leningradsky Railroad Station	262-4281
Paveletsky Railroad Station	235-4673
Rizhsky Railroad Station	266-1176
Savyolovsky Railroad Station	285-9000
Yaroslavsky Railroad Station	266-0595
Reservation Information	262-6791
Reservations	266-8333

River Travel

Northern River Terminal	457-4050
Southern River Terminal	118-7955

Local Transportation

Taxis (to order)	225-0000
	227-0040
Car rental center (at Cosmos Hotel)	215-6191

Lost and Found

Taxi	233-4225
Metro	222-2085
Tram, trolley bus or bus	923-8753

Hotels

Cosmos	217-0785
Intourist	203-4008
Telex	411823
Metropol	225-6677
Mezhdunarodnaya	253-7729
Telex	411486

National	203-6539
Rossiya	298-5400
Savoy	225-6910
Ukraina	243-3021
Belgrad	248-6692/1643
Berlin	221-0477
Budapest	924-8820
Varshava	238-1970
Dom Turista	434-2782
Druzhba	432-9629
Izmailovo	166-0109
Leningradskaya	208-2008
Minsk	299-1211
Mozhaiskaya	447-3434
Molodezhnaya	210-4565
Moskva	292-1000
Orlyonok	939-8844
Ostankino	219-2880
Pekin	209-2442
Salyut	438-6565
Sevastopol	110-4659
Sovetskaya	250-2342
Solnechny	119-7100
Soyuz	457-9004
Sport	131-1191
Sputnik	125-7106
Yunost	242-1980

Foreign Embassies

Australia, 13 Kropotkinsky Pereulok	246-5012/16
	241-2035/36
Brazil, 54 Ulitsa Gertsena	290-4022–26
Canada, 23 Starokonyushenny Pereulok	241-5882/
	5070/4407
Finland, 15-17 Kropotkinsky Pereulok	246-4027
	230 2592/2143/4
France, 43, 45-47 Ulitsa Dimitrova	236-0003
	231-8501

Germany (FRG), 17 Ulitsa Bolshaya Gruzinskaya	252-5521
Italy, 5 Ulitsa Vesnina	241-1533/36
Japan, 12 Kalashny Pereulok	291-8500/01
Mexico, 4 Ulitsa Schukina	201-4848
Netherlands, 6 Kalashny Pereulok	291-2999/ 2948/2954/2976
New Zealand, 44 Ulitsa Vorovskovo	290-3485/ 1277/5704
Sweden, 60 Ulitsa Mosfilmovskaya	147-9009
Switzerland, 2/5 Pereulok Stopani	925-5322/ 6930
United Kingdom, 14 Maurice Thorez Embankment	231-8511/12
United States, 19-21-23 Ulitsa Chaykovskovo	252-2451/59

Communications Services

International telephone exchange
(for placing calls to other countries)   333-4101

Information (for calls within the U.S.S.R.)   07

International Couriers
Barry Martin Travel, Room 940
Mezhdunarodnaya Hotel   253-2940

Chambers of Commerce

Moscow Chamber of Commerce	299-7612
American Soviet Trade and Economic Council	243-4028/5621/ 5470/5495/5228
British-Soviet Chamber of Commerce	253-2554
Franco-Soviet Chamber of Commerce	208-9351
Finnish-Soviet Chamber of Commerce	925-9001
Italian-Soviet Chamber of Commerce	241-6517

THE BUSINESS CLIMATE IN MOSCOW:
AN OVERVIEW

Whenever promising new markets are discovered, there is a tendency to overreact: opportunities for tapping new sources of goods, or exploiting new consumer markets, can be exaggerated. The voyages of Christopher Columbus were motivated and financed by the quest for gold, and for new routes to sources of the spice trade. Nineteenth-century British traders are said to have cherished the hope that a half-billion Chinese could be coaxed into adding an inch to the length of their cotton gowns, a change that would have kept the mills at Birmingham spinning around the clock. Although those particular expectations were not met, pioneers of those days discovered other opportunities and possibilities, sometimes far more important. Business pioneers in our time, too, have often found that while particular goals and expectations were not met, they led to even greater, unexpected opportunities.

For international business in this last decade of the 20th century, the reordering of the politics and economics of the Soviet Union will have profound effects. The transformation of the Soviet Union under Mikhail

Gorbachev's reforms — changes that have also shaken
and transformed Eastern Europe — have sent Pentagon
strategists and corporate planners alike scurrying for
ways to deal with new realities and, very likely, important opportunities. Chances are that the children and
grandchildren of the readers of this book will reap whatever benefits there are from the evolving opportunities
for trade with the Soviet Union. Nevertheless, the special
opportunities for pioneering these new territories are
unfolding now, and today's entrepreneurs are in the
unique position of being offered a Soviet economy that
is in transition and is almost completely reshaping itself.

The Soviet Union is moving toward a market-
oriented replacement for the failed economic experiment
in collectivism that has lasted nearly three quarters of
a century. Moscow has opened its doors not only to allow,
but also to encourage, foreign participation in the economic reformation of the U.S.S.R. The Soviet economy is
made up of 285 million people who lack nearly everything: not only such items as televisions, video cassette
recorders, cameras, watches, radios, audio cassettes, re-
frigerators and microwave ovens, which are taken for
granted in most developed countries, but also adequate
supplies of such basic necessities as fish, meat, vegetables, fruit, shelter, clothing and medical care. Soviet
consumers represent a potential market for just about
everything a foreign business can offer.

Although the Soviet Union is severely lacking in
consumer goods, it is not lacking in natural resources.
In terms of land mass, the U.S.S.R. is the largest country in the world. This expanse includes more extensive
natural resources than those of any other country: vast
deposits of gold, silver, diamonds, platinum, chromium
and other rare and valuable metals and minerals; stands
of timber the size of all of North America; huge petroleum and natural gas reserves; vast areas for the development of agriculture, industry and fisheries; and a very
significant potential for the development of tourism.
Moscow is the city in which commercial transactions
concerning all of these resources take place.

WHAT KIND OF BUSINESS IS POSSIBLE?

Not surprisingly, the Soviets are encouraging foreign
interest in doing business with them by creating policies

and a legal framework within which to work. It is equally unsurprising that, at this stage at least, the Soviets are encouraging the kind of foreign business involvement that they believe will best suit the needs of the Soviet Union. Thus, the business alternatives now open in the U.S.S.R. are not always those that best meet the objectives of foreign buyers, sellers and investors.

Joint Ventures. The first Soviet legislation designed to attract foreign investment was the joint venture decree, which was promulated on January 13, 1987. Under Soviet law, a joint venture is a single legal entity co-owned and jointly managed by one or more Soviet and foreign business partners. It is clear from Soviet legislation and policy statements that the intended purposes of joint ventures in the U.S.S.R. are to attract foreign capital, equipment, know-how, management experience and marketing techniques in order to earn foreign exchange from the production of new or improved products or services for export. The Soviet party, over a fixed term, will gain whatever an experienced business partner can offer. At the end of the term of the venture, the business will in most instances continue as the property of the Soviet party. Clearly, if it works according to plan, a joint venture can help the Soviet Union achieve the innovation, productivity and prosperity that have proved so illusive since the October Revolution, and which seemed to have slipped even further away during the years between World War II and Gorbachev's succession — years that the Soviets themselves call "the years of stagnation."

Although they are self-serving, the Soviet joint venture objectives are often compatible with the goals of foreign investors, at least insofar as those investors might be seeking a new base for the production of goods or services. If the U.S.S.R. can become a dependable source of comparatively inexpensive raw materials and labor, and a reliable supplier of quality goods, it will become a desirable base for joint ventures. There are significant obstacles, however, and they should not be discounted. There is already very significant competition for the foreign investor's dollar in countries that offer a skilled and reliable labor force producing quality goods at competitive costs. The U.S.S.R. today is no Taiwan, Hong Kong, South Korea, Singapore or Thailand. Eastern Europe, too, promises to become a competitor with the Soviet Union for foreign investment.

Foreign investors are often willing to participate in a joint venture in the U.S.S.R. because they think that it is the only way of gaining a foothold in the Soviet Union for later entry into the Soviet domestic market. This is a natural tendency, considering the massive unmet needs in the Soviet economy in nearly every imaginable category. But a prudent foreign investor will take care to be certain that projections for a joint venture, standing alone, are economically sound. A loss leader may be just that, a leader to future losses.

Despite the fact that it has been closed to foreign investment until recently, the U.S.S.R. has not been totally isolated from world trade. On the contrary, the Soviet Union has been an important exporter of metals, minerals, petroleum, petrochemicals, chemicals, forest and marine products, heavy machinery, capital goods and advanced technology. It has also been a buyer of advanced equipment, machinery and agricultural products from abroad. Although Soviet trade with Eastern Europe and other socialist countries has predominated, the U.S.S.R. has also carried on commerce with Japan, Western Europe and the U.S. Buying and selling activity with the West and with Japan is certain to increase as the current reforms take hold.

Sales to the U.S.S.R. Those companies interested in sales to the U.S.S.R. must contend with the fact that the Soviet Union, from a foreign-exchange-reserve point of view, is a poor country. Hard currency is available only for priority imports; therefore, many would-be exporters will have to come up with imaginative plans for barter-like transactions to make their sales possible. PepsiCo, Inc., for example, one of the genuine success stories of developing business in the Soviet Union, finances the expansion of its bottling plants and Pizza Hut outlets in the U.S.S.R. by barter trade in Stolichnaya Vodka, and even Soviet ships, accepting such products in payment for some of its goods and services.

Another important consideration is U.S. export regulations. Sellers of high-tech products or processes must, for the foreseeable future, be certain that their proposed sales are permitted by U.S. export regulations, even as we see those regulations begin to relax.

Buying from the U.S.S.R. Buyers, at least in the U.S., must take into account that U.S. tariffs on imports from the U.S.S.R. have historically been so high as to wipe out landed cost advantages. This is the result of U.S. legislation known as the Jackson-Vanik Amendment to the Trade Act of 1974. Jackson-Vanik denies certain trade benefits, including the most-favored-nation tariff treatment, on imports from the U.S.S.R. as long as Congress or the President believes that the Soviet Union interferes unduly with its citizens' freedom to emigrate. The Jackson-Vanik Amendment can be waived, and the tariff problem can be addressed in a bilateral trade agreement, but the ever-present possibility exists that frictions in U.S.-Soviet relations (such as those occurring in 1990 over Lithuania) might prompt the U.S. to reimpose discriminatory tariffs. The quality of Soviet products will need improvement before they are suitable for foreign markets, although a parallel experience with China since the early 1970's indicates that product quality and productivity can be achieved where there is sufficient determination to be competitive.

When ruptures in the political relationship between the U.S. and the U.S.S.R. have occurred in the past, as at the time of the Soviet invasion of Afghanistan, they have had a profoundly negative effect on trade and commerce. Though such events might seem unlikely in the current climate of reform and good will, they are not impossible. Protection against such a possibility, or against the chance of domestic problems in the U.S.S.R. that could disrupt trade or business, can never be foolproof; however, these potential hazards should be addressed in contracts, in practical limitations on exposure (such as prudent levels of investment or credit), and with insurance (such as that offered against political risk by OPIC or other, private, carriers).

MAKING CONTACT

Establishing contact with Soviet enterprises is becoming more complex as reforms of the trade apparatus continue. Foreign trade in the U.S.S.R. is no longer monopolized by Foreign Trade Organizations (FTOs), which functioned until 1986, under the Ministry of Foreign Trade. That Ministry, in fact, has itself been reorganized into the Ministry of Foreign Economic Relations. Today, all of the Soviet ministries, some two dozen of them, have the right to engage directly in transactions with foreign parties. Moreover, state committees, privately owned cooperatives and large state enterprises also have the right to engage in foreign trade without using an FTO as an intermediary.

A foreign firm wishing to do business in the U.S.S.R. must first solve the daunting problem of identifying and making contact with a prospective business partner. A number of the Moscow-based organizations that may be contacted for assistance in identifying a possible business partner are listed in the following sections.

Vneshekonombank. This office provides currency to enterprises for financing export-import operations, and supervises the foreign economic operations of the specialized banks of the Soviet Union.

Bank for Foreign Economic Relations
  (Vneshekonombank)
37 Ulitsa Plushchikha
Moscow 119121
Tel.: 246-6780, 246-6788, 246-6798
Telex: 411174, 411904, 411453

The Ministry of Finance of the U.S.S.R. The Finance Ministry oversees balance of payments plans and regulates credits given to enterprises to develop export production facilities. It is the Soviet organ responsible for the registration of joint ventures.

Ministry of Finance of the U.S.S.R.
Protocol Department
9 Ulitsa Kuibysheva
Moscow 103097
Tel.: Foreign Relations Dept., 223-4511
    Information, 298-9191

U.S.-U.S.S.R. Trade and Economic Council. This Council, sometimes referred to as ASTEC or USTEC, is a membership organization whose members include both U.S. and Soviet enterprises. It has two offices, one in New York, the other in Moscow. The Council draws some 500 business representatives to its annual membership meetings, which are held alternately in the U.S. and the U.S.S.R. The 1989 annual meeting occurred in Moscow in May. The Council refuses to disclose the names of its member firms, but it is known that most large U.S. companies that do business in the Soviet Union are members. The Council's directorates and professional staff positions are held by approximately equal numbers of U.S. and Soviet nationals.

Although the Council has been faulted for its high annual dues and scant services to U.S. member firms, its Moscow office (located within a short walk of the Ukraina Hotel) does offer very useful member services, including a bilingual professional staff; work areas for visiting representatives of member firms; and conference rooms available for technical discussions, negotiations and product or catalogue exhibitions.

U.S.-U.S.S.R. Trade and Economic Council
3 Shevchenko Embankment
Moscow
Tel.: 243-4028
Telex: 413212 (ASTEC SU)

Intourist. This agency reports to the State Committee for Foreign Tourism. Intourist organizes travel itineraries for foreign tourists through a series of departments organized along geographic or national lines. It operates hotels and restaurants throughout the Soviet Union.

Intourist
16 Marx Prospect
Moscow
Tel.: 203-6962
Telex: 411211

Soviet Customs. This office oversees and verifies that all shipments entering the Soviet Union meet with customs regulations.

Soviet Main Customs Administration
9 Komsomolskaya Ploshchad, 1a
Moscow 107140
Tel.: Protocol Office, 208-2441
      Information, 208-4462

Expocentre. Expocentre organizes and sponsors most exhibitions in the U.S.S.R. It offers a variety of publicity arrangements, service facilities and hotel accommodations. Expocentre's business activities are handled by its own professionals and by staff members from the Ministry of Foreign Economic Relations.

Expocentre
1a Sokolnichesky Val
Moscow 107113
Tel.: 268-5874
Telex: 411185 (EXPO SU)

Vneshekonomservice. This office provides various services to foreign enterprises on a commercial basis. These services include legal consultation, assistance in drafting documents, arbitration, finance and accounting advice, statistical studies and market research services, as well as economic analytic services and cost effectiveness studies for a variety of joint projects.

Vneshekonomservice
6 Ulitsa Kuibysheva
Moscow 103735
Tel.: 925-3529
Telex: 411431 (TPP SU)

U.S.S.R. Chamber of Commerce and Industry. This non-governmental organization promotes the development of trade and economic, scientific and technical relations between the Soviet Union and other countries.

U.S.S.R. Chamber of
    Commerce and Industry
6 Ulitsa Kuibysheva
Moscow 103684
Tel.: 923-4323
Telex: 411126

Other Sources. The following offices can also be contacted for assistance in establishing contact with businesses:

Protocol Department
    Ministry of Foreign
    Economic Relations
    of the U.S.S.R.
32/34 Smolenskaya
    Sennaya
Moscow 121200
Tel.: 244-3480

State Foreign Economic
    Commission of the
    Council of Ministers
    of the U.S.S.R.
P.O. Box 9
22a Gorky Street
Moscow 103050
Tel.: 203-9000

U.S.S.R. Committee
    on Science
    and Technology
Ulitsa Gorkogo, 11
Moscow
Tel.: 229-2000
Telex: 411241

CONDUCTING BUSINESS IN MOSCOW

AGENTS AND INTERMEDIARIES

A combination of factors has resulted in a profusion of
business agents and intermediaries in both the U.S. and
the U.S.S.R. offering their services to companies
interested in developing projects in the Soviet Union.
Primary among these factors is the labyrinthine
bureaucracy for which the U.S.S.R. is famous; the whole-
sale restructuring of that bureaucracy that has been
underway for several years; the scarcity of any dependable directory of, or compendium of information about,
Soviet enterprises and government organizations; the
comparative freedom of Soviet entrepreneurs to organize
cooperative service organizations; the number of
educated émigrés from the U.S.S.R. now living in the U.S.
who are eager to capitalize on their knowledge of the
Russian language and Soviet ways; and the always alert
private sector in the U.S. that has made consultative
services an industry unto itself.

The nature of the services available varies widely.
Some service organizations assist with every aspect of
a business, from identifying potential business partners

to providing services to your joint venture. Others offer such particular services as translation, interpretation, information gathering, marketing strategies, personnel training, publications and seminars.

It is beyond the scope of this book to list or rate the organizations offering business services. A major problem with such groups is that they are often short-lived. Some, of course, are long-standing, highly reputable organizations that have simply added their Soviet expertise to a broad range of services. In place of a list, the following suggestions should guide you if you require outside assistance:

1. Ask your prospective agent, intermediary, consultant — even your prospective legal counsel or banker — for references; you are entitled to know if they have done this kind of work before and, if so, for whom.

2. Get an estimate of the charges involved for each discrete aspect of the work to be done.

3. If you are considering engaging a business representative for the U.S.S.R. to act as a commission agent, be sure of the following:

   • Be certain the agreement with the agent is made on the basis of a written contract; unwritten understandings, on the basis of which an enterprising representative will undertake discussions on your behalf, are an invitation to real trouble.

   • Review the agent's list of clients or at least obtain a written assurance that it does not include any of your competitors.

   • Your agent is presumably selling an ability to help you succeed, so try to fix compensation on the basis of success achieved — if possible, solely on the basis of a commission for sales actually made, or a project successfully undertaken. If a monthly retainer must be paid, try to keep it low, and as an advance against any future commissions payable.

   • Every agent has expenses, and you will very likely be expected to cover money advanced for what your agent does for your company alone (e.g., travel and telecommunication expenses). Control these expenses by setting a ceiling on what expenses the agent can incur without first obtaining your approval.

- Most agents want exclusivity, that is, they want to be your sole representative for a fixed period of time. If you are willing to agree to an exclusive arrangement, be certain it does not foreclose your company from seeking to make contacts in the U.S.S.R. on its own.

- Provide terms for cancelling your agent's services with or without cause, at your sole discretion. Don't invite a lawsuit about whether you had sufficient grounds to end the relationship. At the same time, be sure that the contract is clear and fair on the subject of commissions earned before termination of the agreement (though perhaps payable later).

- Require activity reports, if not progress reports, to be sure that your agent hasn't gone to sleep on your project.

MARKET RESEARCH

The same conditions that give rise to the need for consulting or agency services in the U.S.S.R. create a need for information about the Soviet market for your goods, services or technology. To some extent, your need for market information can be met by a good business representative. You should look for additional information about the Soviet market from the Soviet and U.S. government agencies listed in this book, and from your industry trade association. Other good sources of information are the conferences and seminars about the U.S.S.R. that are being held with increasing frequency; publications of the organizations listed elsewhere in this book; trade shows in the U.S.S.R. as well as shows abroad to which the Soviets customarily send observers; and trade missions between the two countries. In addition, don't overlook the daily newspaper as an important source of information that may bear directly on plans for business in the Soviet Union.

Remember, too, that the federal government is not the only source of governmental assistance available in the U.S. Many states have already organized trade missions to the Soviet Union, led by state trade promotion officials. Illinois has gone so far as to open a trade promotion office in Moscow. Your state or city may be a sister to a Soviet republic or city. Where such relationships exist, business prospects are often brighter than they would be in other parts of the Soviet Union.

THE BUSINESS PROPOSAL

If your business proposal is one that has been invited by a Soviet organization, be sure to respond directly and fully to the questions you have been asked. In most instances, though, you will not have an inquiry from a Soviet organization. Instead, you will want to know whether or not there is a market for your goods or services in the Soviet Union and, if so, how to identify interested parties. Some ideas for making contact with interested Soviet parties are contained in the "Making Contact" section of this book. In addition, here are some suggestions for fashioning a business proposal designed to elicit interest from Soviet enterprises:

- Prepare a proposal designed especially for the Soviet audience; it is not enough to simply slap a cover letter onto existing literature. At the same time, this need not be an expensive proposition. A typewritten proposal enclosed in a soft-covered binder is perfectly acceptable.

- The business proposal and all companion documents or pictures should be combined into a single document. This will reduce the possibility of pieces of the package being mislaid.

- Print the principal text of the proposal in both Russian and English. This will add to the expense, but it will also add to the proposal's usefulness. Imagine how your company would respond to a proposal from a Soviet organization written entirely in Russian.

- Describe what type of business you are interested in doing in the U.S.S.R. Keep in mind that you must be clear about your interests, but you don't want to close the door on other ideas that might have occurred to a Soviet enterprise but did not occur to you.

- Invite inquiries from interested parties, and be sure that complete instructions for reaching you by telex, fax and telephone are given in the proposal. Be prepared to follow up the inquiries you do receive, e.g., proposing that representatives of the responding party meet your representatives in Moscow for preliminary talks.

- Prepare numerous copies of this proposal, and circulate it as widely as you can. Even the printing of 100 copies for circulation in the Soviet Union will likely cost far less than a single business trip.

ADVERTISING IN THE SOVIET UNION

While advertising foreign products in the Soviet Union is no longer unheard-of, it is still in its infancy. PepsiCo, Inc., has not only bought Soviet television time for its ads, but it has filmed such spots in the U.S.S.R. With such agencies as BBD&O establishing joint ventures in the Soviet Union, the opportunity — or the necessity — for advertising there is not far off.

LEGAL SERVICES

The decrees and legislation designed to encourage foreign investment in the Soviet Union are amounting to a considerable body of law. Consequently, lawyers are necessary when your business planning is beyond the stage of informal rumination. Various Soviet agencies make quasi-legal services available. For example, Vneshekonomservice offers copies of Soviet laws and advice about documenting foreign trade and joint venture transactions.

For U.S. legal services to U.S. companies, the authors of this book are understandably biased toward Baker & McKenzie, the world's largest law firm with some 1,500 lawyers and 49 offices throughout the world. Its Moscow office, staffed by Russian-speaking attorneys, is located near Pushkin Square, just off Gorky Street and about midway between McDonald's and Pizza Hut. The firm's address is:

Baker & McKenzie
Pushkin Plaza
Bolshoi Gnezdnykovsky Pereulok 7
Moscow
Tel.:   200-6167, 200-4906, 200-6186
Fax: 200-0203
Telex: 413671 (BAKER SU)

Inquiries to Baker & McKenzie from within the U.S. can be addressed to Eugene Theroux, one of the authors of this book, at the firm's Washington office. The firm's address is:

Baker & McKenzie
815 Connecticut Avenue, N.W.
Washington, D.C. 20006
Tel.:202-452-7000
Fax: 202-452-7074
Telex: 89552 (ABOGADO WSH)

Inquiries can also be sent to Soviet law specialists in the firm's offices in Chicago and New York:

Baker & McKenzie
One Prudential Plaza
Chicago, Illinois 60601
Tel.: 312-861-8000
Fax: 312-861-2898
James T. Hitch, III
Preston M. Torbert

Baker & McKenzie
805 Third Avenue
New York, NY 10022
Tel.: 212-751-5700
Fax: 212-759-9133
Charles J. Conroy

In addition to Baker & McKenzie, several other firms have lawyers in Moscow. They include Coudert Brothers and Steptoe & Johnson. You may also find that the law firm that already assists your company on international matters has developed an in-house capability for Soviet-related work.

BANKING SERVICES

Aproximately 50 foreign banks have established resident representative offices in Moscow. While these offices are not authorized to conduct ordinary banking services in Moscow, they can be valuable sources of advice on banking matters relating to trade and investment. Two such banks are:

Bank of America NT & SA,
the U.S.A.
Room 1605, 12 Krasnopres-
nenskaya Embankment.
The Moscow World Trade
Center
Tel.: 253-7054
253-1910
253-1911
Telex: 413189

The Chase Manhattan
Bank N.A. the U.S.A.
Room 1709, 12 Krasnopres-
nenskaya Embankment.
The Moscow World Trade
Center
Tel.: 230-2174
253-1496
253-8377
Telex: 413912

The two Soviet banks principally concerned with transactions involving foreigners are:

**The State Bank of the U.S.S.R.
(Gosbank S.S.S.R.)**

12 Niglinnaya Ulitsa,
Moscow 103016
Tel.: 923-2038

The State Bank of the U.S.S.R. is the major organ in the Soviet banking community. It supervises the centralized management of the money and credit system of the country and is responsible for the uniform state credit policy, coordination of the activity of Soviet banks, organization of interbank settlements, consolidation of money circulation and cash performance of the state budget, and participates in the shaping of the master currency plan of the country.

The State Bank of the U.S.S.R. is the accrediting body for those foreign banks that express an intention of opening their representations in the Soviet Union.

The Bank for Foreign Economic Affairs of the U.S.S.R. (Vneshekonombank S.S.S.R.)

37 Ulitsa Plushchikha,
Moscow 119121
Tel.: 246-6731, 227-0253

Vneshekonombank is responsible for the organizing and effecting of settlements on import, export and noncommercial transactions, the crediting of foreign trade associations, enterprises and organizations; supervises the fulfillment of the master currency plan of the country, and the rational and economical utilization of hard currency funds; effects transactions on international money and capital markets and payments involving foreign currencies and valuables.

ACCOUNTING SERVICES

Like the large law firms, the major international accounting firms, including Ernst & Young, Price Waterhouse, Arthur Anderson and Coopers & Lybrand maintain offices in Moscow. They, too, are a source of important advice and assistance to their visiting clients.

SOURCES OF ASSISTANCE FOR TRADING WITH THE U.S.S.R

U.S. Government Sources in the U.S.

Department of Commerce. Several bureaus of this department can be of assistance. **The Joint US. - U.S.S.R. Commercial Commission** (JCC) was established as an official body at the Moscow Summit in May 1972 to negotiate commercial agreements and to oversee their implementation. The Commission, which normally convenes at least once a year, is the mechanism for commercial dialogue between the two countries at both the policy and staff levels; it is also a forum for problem-solving and discussion of operational matters.

The JCC's meetings are alternately held in Moscow and Washington, D.C. The mission of the 1988 JCC, held in Moscow, was to demonstrate U.S. interest in increasing trade in non-strategic areas, as well as to carry out President Reagan's and General Secretary Gorbachev's instructions from the December Summit to develop concrete steps for expanding trade and economic relations. Advances were made in developing ways for American companies to get the information needed to explore new possibilities resulting from both Soviet trade reforms and the Department of Commerce's expanded trade promotion program. The 1989 JCC, convened in Washington, concerned itself with a U.S.-Soviet trade agreement and related issues.

One result of JCC activity has been the establishment of five bilateral sectoral working groups that identify opportunities and eliminate obstacles to development of business in the fields of medical equipment, construction equipment, oil and gas equipment, and equipment for the consumer-goods and food-processing industries. These groups form an ongoing channel for obtaining improved information on commercial possibilities arising as Soviet industry develops, and for getting quick responses to U.S. companies' inquiries.

The U.S.S.R. Division, International Trade Administration provides policy guidance; current information and analysis of economic developments, foreign trade policy and commercial practices in the U.S.S.R.; help with Soviet foreign trade contracts; and information on Commerce-sponsored trade promotion activities in the Soviet Union. Its staff keeps abreast of relevant developments, and is responsible for substantive and secretariat support for the JCC, as well as contact with the U.S. Commercial Office in Moscow and with Soviet commercial offices in the U.S. The address is:

U.S. Department of Commerce
Room 3413, Herbert Hoover Building
Washington, D.C. 20230
Tel.: 202-377-4655

The Bureau of Export Administration (BXA) should be consulted before beginning negotiations on exports to the Soviet Union, in order to clarify applicable export control policies and regulations. The Department of Commerce administers export controls for national security, foreign policy, or short supply reasons. The Commodity Control List (part 799.1 of the Export Administration Regulations) states which commodities require a validated license for export to the Soviet Union. A validated export license is a document issued by BXA authorizing a specific item for a specific end use in a specific country. If no license is required, the exporter simply indicates on the shipper's export declaration that the items are exportable under General License "G-DEST."

Specific questions or requests for assistance should be addressed to:

Exporter Service Staff
Bureau of Export Administration
U.S. Department of Commerce
Washington, DC 20230
202-377-4811

U.S. firms contemplating joint ventures with the Soviet Union can receive counseling from BXA. Early counseling regarding export licensing for U.S.-Soviet joint venture proposals and related technology transfers is advisable. Interested parties should contact Mr. Sandy Dhier, Director of the Capital Branch of BXA, at 202-377-5695

For firms interested in purchasing Soviet-origin goods, the **Office of Import Investigations** can identify restrictions on imports from the U.S.S.R., and has up-to-date information on the status of dumping and countervailing duty investigations. The International Trade Administration is responsible for determining whether foreign merchandise is being sold in the U.S. at less than fair value according to the Tariff Act of 1930. The International Trade Commission is responsible for determining whether these sales injure U.S. industry. In the event that both investigations show that a foreign country or firm is indeed dumping products in the U.S. market, an importer is required to deposit estimated dumping duties on all merchandise subject to affirmative action. The Office of Import Investigations' address is:

U.S. Department of Commerce
Room 3047, Herbert Hoover Building
Washington, DC 20230
Tel.: 202-377-5497

Firms interested in importing from the U.S.S.R. can contact the Government Printing Office at 202-783-3238 to purchase the Tariff Schedule of the United States, Annotated (TSUSA) 1987, USITC #1910, for information on U.S. tariff rates for foreign goods. Many large libraries will have the TSUSA schedules as well. At this writing, the U.S. does not extend Most-Favored-Nation (MFN) status to the Soviet Union, so look under column 2 for imports to determine the tariff rate. Also note that a U.S.-Soviet trade agreement, expected to be signed at a June 1990 summit meeting by President Bush and President Gorbachev, may contain provisions for MFN tariff treatment.

Department of Agriculture (USDA). The Foreign Agricultural Service (FAS) has several Washington offices that will accept calls regarding trade opportunities for specific commodities:

Grains and Feed Division	202-447-6219
Dairy, Livestock and Poultry Division	202-447-8031
Oilseeds and Products Division	202-447-7037
Tobacco, Cotton and Seeds Division	202-382-9516
Horticulture and Tropical Plants Division	202-447-6590

Information regarding U.S. Government Trade Policy and the Export Enhancement Program (EEP) may be obtained from:

The Office of Trade Policy
Africa, Asia and the Middle East Division
Foreign Agricultural Service
U.S. Department of Agriculture
Washington, DC
Tel.:202-382-1289

The EEP is the only U.S. agricultural trade program currently in effect with the U.S.S.R.

Department of State. Two offices at the Department of State are involved in the formulation and implementation of U.S. economic policies vis-à-vis the Soviet Union:

Economic Section
Office of Soviet Union Affairs
Bureau of European Affairs
U.S. Department of State
Washington, DC 20520
202-647-9370

Office of East-West Trade
Bureau of Economic Affairs
U.S. Department of State
Washington, DC 20520
202-647-2875

Other Departments. The political risk and currency inconvertibility insurance programs and other related programs administered by the **Overseas Private Investment Corporation** (OPIC) have been an important stimulus to U.S. private investment in many developing countries. While these programs are not available for projects in the U.S.S.R., pending a trade agreement, it is considered likely that OPIC programs will eventually become available to U.S. businesses for their Soviet projects. This is an independent, self-supporting corporation owned by the U.S. government.

Overseas Private
   Investment Corporation
1615 M Street, N.W.
Washington, DC 20527
Tel.: 202-457-7200
Fax: 202-331-4234

Like those of OPIC, the financing programs of the **Export-Import Bank of the U.S.** (EXIM Bank) are not currently available for projects in the U.S.S.R. The Stevenson Amendment to the Trade Act of 1974 prohibits any agency of the U.S., other than the Commodity Credit Corporation, from approving any loans, guarantees, insurance or any combination thereof, in connection with exports to the Soviet Union in an amount exceeding $300 million without prior Congressional approval. In addition to the restrictions imposed by the Stevenson Amendment, EXIM loans are further restricted by the Export-Import Bank Act of 1945 as amended by the Byrd Amendment of 1974. The Byrd Amendment prohibits EXIM from providing any loan or financial guarantee, or any combination thereof, in an amount exceeding $40 million for the "purchase, lease, or procurement of any product or service which involves research or exploration of fossil fuel energy resources" in the U.S.S.R. This restrictive legislation was enacted more than a decade and a half ago, when U.S.-Soviet relations were at a very different stage, and the Soviet Union itself was a very different place. It is thus

considered reasonably likely that EXIM programs will
become available to U.S. investors in Soviet projects. The
EXIM Bank customarily offers direct loans for large
projects and equipment sales that require long-term
financing. It also guarantees loans made by cooperating
U.S. and foreign commercial buyers of U.S. products and
services.

Export-Import Bank of the U.S.
811 Vermont Avenue, N.W.
Washington, DC 20571

The objective of the **U.S. Trade and Development
Program** (TDP) is to promote both U.S. exports and
economic development. TDP is both a trade and an aid
program; it accomplishes these two objectives by
financing feasibility studies and related planning
services (e.g., conferences and training) for projects in
developing countries. These projects must be important
to a country's development, and must offer good export
opportunities for U.S. equipment and services. The TDP
is not yet authorized for projects in the U.S.S.R., but
under a future U.S.-U.S.S.R. trade agreement it could
become available.

U.S. Trade and Development Program
Room 309, SA-16
Washington, DC 20523
703-875-4357

Soviet Sources in the U.S.

There are several Soviet organizations who are equipped
to assist and advise American companies with respect
to business in the U.S.S.R. They are:

Commercial Section
Embassy of the U.S.S.R.
1125 16th Street, N.W.
Washington, DC 20036

Trade Representation of
   the U.S.S.R. in the U.S.
2001 Connecticut Ave., N.W.
Washington, DC 20008
Tel.: 202-232-5988

AMTORG Trading
   Corporation
1755 Broadway
New York, N.Y. 10019
Tel.: 212-956-3010
Fax: 212-956-2995
Telex: 422400 AMTG

Bank for Foreign
   Economic Relations
("Vneshekonombank")
527 Madison Avenue
New York, NY 10022
Tel.: 212-421-8660
Fax: 212-421-8677
Telex: 6730675

Belarus Machinery Inc.
Suite 1450
115 East 57th Street
New York, NY 10022
Tel.: 212-751-8550

Other Sources in the U.S.

The U.S.-U.S.S.R. Trade and Economic Council. A
general description of the U.S.-U.S.S.R. Trade and
Economic Council is given above, at page **XX**. The
address of the Council's U.S. office is listed here to serve
as a reminder that the Council's services are available
to its members in the U.S. as well as through its Moscow
office.

The U.S.-U.S.S.R. Trade and
    Economic Council
805 Third Avenue
New York, NY 10022
Tel.: 212-644-4550
Fax: 212-752-0889

American Committee on U.S.-Soviet Relations. This
organization is supported by corporate and individual
contributors. Its Washington, D.C., location enables it to
keep abreast of political and legislative developments
affecting bilateral relations. The Committee has an
active trade-related program, consisting of publications
and conferences arranged between Americans and
Soviets with common interests.

American Committee
    on U.S.-Soviet Relations
109 Eleventh Street, S.E.
Washington, DC 20003
Tel.: 202-546-1700

Sources in the U.S.S.R.

The United States maintains offices in Moscow that can
assist American business representatives. Services
available include briefings, and giving advice relating
to contacts with Soviet authorities.

The American Embassy. The Embassy is located in an
old building at Ulitsa Chaikovskovo 19/23. A new
Embassy complex, completed in 1989, has been ordered
destroyed and rebuilt by the U.S. following the discovery
that Soviet agencies had implanted surveillance devices

in the new building. Probably nowhere else in the world do American diplomats work under more stressful conditions than they do in Moscow. This is not only the result of an antiquated building in which officials are squeezed cheek by jowl for lack of sufficient space, but also because of the need for extraordinary security — even in these days of warming U.S.-Soviet relations. All U.S. visitors to the U.S.S.R. are encouraged to register at the Consular Section of the American Embassy upon arrival in Moscow, preferably in person. Besides registration at the Embassy, U.S. business visitors should not expect much in the way of assistance from Embassy officials, who are occupied with the burdensome task of analyzing and reporting on the Soviet economy at a time of awe-inspiring change. Nevertheless, commercial services are available at the Embassy as follows:

Commercial Counselor
Embassy of the U.S.A.
Ulitsa Chaikovskovo 19/23
Moscow
Tel.: 252-2451
    through 252-2459
Telex: 413160 (USGSO SU)

Office of the Agricultural
    Counselor
Embassy of the U.S.A.
Moscow
Tel.: 252-2451
    through 252-2459
Telex: 413160 (USGSO SU)

By Mail:
Agricultural Counselor
American Embassy
Moscow
APO New York, NY 09862

Also located at the Embassy is the Agricultural Office of the foreign Agricultural Service. This bureau of the U.S. Department of Agriculture can assist businesses with information on trade opportunities, current market analyses and crop reports.

The U.S. Commercial Office. The U.S. Department of
Commerce operates the U.S. Commercial Office (USCO)
for policy guidance, trade policy briefings, and assistance
in business facilitation (e.g., arranging meetings,
temporary office space, audiovisual and translation
equipment). The USCO also has a commercial library,
telex and photocopying equipment, and is open weekdays
from 9 AM to 6 PM.

U.S. Commercial Office
James May, Commercial Officer
Maria Aronson, Commercial Attaché
Ulitsa Chaikovskovo 15
Moscow
Tel.: 255-4848
Fax: 230-2101
Telex: 413205 (USCO SU)

By Mail:
U.S. Commercial Office/U.S.S.R.
American Embassy Moscow
APO New York, NY 09862

   Business visitors to Moscow who may also have need
to travel to Leningrad should note that there is a U.S.
Consulate in Leningrad:

Consulate General of the U.S.
15 Ulitsa Petra-Lavrova
Leningrad
Tel.: 292-4548
Telex: 64121527 (AMCONSUL SU)

By Mail:
U.S. Consulate General Leningrad
15 Box L
APO New York, NY 09664-5440

VI

JOINT VENTURES

Foreign business visitors to the Soviet Union these days are nearly bowled over by what they perceive to be an enormous potential for trade and investment. Political conditions have never been more favorable. Soviet planners speak enthusiastically of the U.S.S.R.'s drive toward a "regulated market economy." The need for improvement in all kinds of goods and services could not be more apparent.

Your interest in doing business will be more than reciprocated on the Soviet side. Soviet enterprises that encounter foreign firms are very likely—often in the very first informal discussion—to propose a joint business venture. Ever alert to new opportunities, foreign business visitors are often surprised to discover not only that sales and purchases are possible, but that direct investment is, too. In fact Soviet law permits a foreign party to own up to 99% of a Soviet joint venture, allows the management of the enterprise to be placed under the direction of a foreign national, and encourages such ventures with tax holidays and other incentives.

Soviet legislation was enacted in 1987 permitting equity joint ventures with foreigners. This law is such a radical departure from Soviet policy that many Soviets and foreigners have come to regard joint ventures as the only reasonable basis for their business transactions. They tend to forget that ordinary import and export transactions are also simplified in the new economic and political atmosphere. Barred since 1917 from direct investment in the Soviet Union, many foreign businesses respond euphorically at the prospect of establishing themselves in the U.S.S.R. Now that they are no longer discouraged from contact with foreigners, Soviet enterprises are equally enthusiastic at the possibility of investments with experienced foreign partners.

While joint ventures are an important framework for doing business, they are also among the most difficult to negotiate and operate. If your firm's management has shied away from undertaking a joint venture with a partner at home, you should think carefully before proposing a joint venture with a Soviet party. In the U.S.S.R. you will encounter great differences in such areas as language, law, custom, worker habits, pricing, taxation, accounting principles, record keeping, labor-management relations and dispute resolution. The ruble's nonconvertibility alone is a daunting problem. And bridging these difficulties is not made easier by the distances between your corporate headquarters and the offices of your Soviet partner—distances that increase the cost and complexity of travel and communication.

Difficulties aside, joint ventures do offer a foreign business an opportunity—unprecedented in this century—to become established on Soviet territory, poised to take advantage of developing opportunities in the U.S.S.R. and benefiting from the protection and encouragement of Soviet law. When each side is satisfied that a joint venture between them makes economic sense, negotiations are the next step.

PRELIMINARY
JOINT VENTURE NEGOTIATIONS

As in nearly all other business negotiations with the Soviets, discussions on joint ventures usually take place in the U.S.S.R. and are normally conducted in the English language on the basis of contract documents prepared in English. The Soviet side ordinarily provides interpreters. The quality of interpretation is unpredictable, however, particularly where technical and legal terms are concerned. Therefore, if it is possible, supply your own interpreter. Of course, usually only the larger foreign firms can afford to bring interpreters from outside the U.S.S.R. In any event, you may be surprised at how well Soviet officials speak English.

PROTOCOLS AND
LETTERS OF INTENT

Considering the time and expense of conducting meetings in Moscow, careful preparation is obviously warranted for every meeting, right from the start. Many firms will not send representatives to a meeting in Moscow until the Soviet side has given a clear and satisfactory written expression of its plans or expectations, and confirmed by telex or fax its agreement to a proposed agenda of topics to be discussed.

After the first meetings have been held, it is useful to both sides if the results of the discussion are set down in a "Letter of Intent" or a "Protocol," which is then signed by the senior representative of each side. If time permits, these should be done both in English and in Russian. If time does not permit, the foreign party should ensure that an English language protocol is prepared; it is rare for the Soviet side to object to this.

There are no prescribed forms for a protocol, letter of intent, or memorandum of understanding. These are not legally binding agreements. They need not be lengthy; usually up to five double-spaced typewritten pages are sufficient. When drafting them, keep in mind that they are road maps for an eventual contract. They can serve such important purposes as setting forth the basic objectives on which the parties are mutually agreed; recording the principal decisions reached at meetings; setting a schedule of events to be followed in preparation for the next phase; and establishing a date, place and agenda for the next meeting. A protocol can be used, for example, to specify which party is to prepare the first draft of a joint venture agreement and charter, how responsibility will be allocated for an initial draft of the feasibility study, and what methods will be used for exchanging views on these various drafts.

In the course of negotiations, several protocols may be adopted as the goals and tasks of the parties are refined. Such a chain of protocols is useful because it keeps the upper echelons of both parties informed about the status and progress of the talks between their representatives.

TECHNICAL TALKS AND THE FEASIBILITY STUDY

When it is evident from preliminary negotiations, as reflected in a protocol or letter of intent, that there is a meeting of the minds, it is time to sit down to exchange the technical information basic to the proposed joint venture agreement and charter. This process almost always takes longer than either side anticipates, and usually requires a series of visits to the Soviet Union over a period of months.

Technical Talks. It is almost inevitable that the exchange of technical data will include, at least indirectly, commercial questions. Thus, while they are often held at separate times and involve different personnel, it is important for both sides that at least some of the people involved in the commercial aspects of the transaction be present for the technical discussions. This not only provides continuity, but helps prevent misunderstandings when the time comes for expressing the intentions of the parties in a written agreement.

What the Soviet may lack in commercial experience they often make up for with technical sophistication. The engineers or other technical specialists you will meet in the U.S.S.R. can be impressive. They have been out of touch with the nonsocialist world, to be sure, but they are avid readers of technical journals. They are likely to be familiar with your technology, and that of your competitors. For your talks and for your written documentation, keep in mind that export control regulations administered by the Coordinating Committee for Multilateral Export Control (COCOM) may restrict the extent to which you may disclose technical data, even at preliminary discussion stages. Also, remember that the U.S.S.R. has adopted the metric system.

Feasibility Studies. Among the important tasks to be performed early in the negotiation process is the completion of a feasibility study that demonstrates the viability of the joint venture. This document is a necessary part of the application for approval of the joint venture by Soviet authorities. It is also a means by which the two parties can identify and rectify defects in their business plan, evolve projections for profitability and outputs, and assess overall whether their proposed joint enterprise has a realistic chance of success. While the content of the feasibility study will vary depending on the nature of the proposed joint venture, attention to the following points will appear in most such studies:

- Identification of the parties to the project, together with their respective areas of competence.

- Summary of the purpose and scope of the venture.

- Description of the compatibility of the venture's objectives with Soviet economic goals.

- Projections on production, marketing and sales of the venture's goods or services.

- Financial plans, including the respective contributions of the parties to the venture; methods of dealing with problems created by the nonconvertible ruble; pricing of goods or services; calculation of profits, dividends or royalties; profit sharing mechanisms; repatriation of payments to the foreign party; tax issues; accounting procedures; the extent to which start-up costs, including the feasibility study itself, will be chargeable to the parties; and an assessment of any need for borrowing.

- Identification of machinery, equipment, raw materials and other inputs needed for the venture, and plans for obtaining these from within the Soviet Union or from abroad.

- Layout of the facility for the production of goods or services.

- Proposed management and operation of the venture, including organization and responsibilities of Soviet and foreign personnel at the managerial, technical and staff levels.

- Description of the nature and composition of the labor force required for the venture.

- Planned schedule for implementation of the venture.

- Summary section containing a discussion giving reasons supporting approval of the project.

Soviet Visitors. Before a final agreement is reached, it is not uncommon for the Soviet side to request an opportunity to travel abroad for a visit to facilities at which your technology, manufacturing methods or other qualifications as a prospective joint venture partner may be observed first hand. This is often a valuable undertaking because it allows the Soviet side's representatives to see for themselves what might be involved in the joint venture to be established in the U.S.S.R. If your company wants or is willing to arrange such a visit, careful planning is essential to prevent it from becoming an unduly expensive or counterproductive junket. Note that here, as with any phase of the negotiations that involves foreign currency costs, the Soviet side can be expected to remind you that the ruble will buy them little or nothing in New York, Milwaukee or Peoria. You will be expected to pick up most of the tab for such a visit, perhaps with the exception of Aeroflot air travel by the Soviet visitors to the city nearest your installation. Obviously, you should build into the joint venture financial structure a reimbursement mechanism for such expenditures.

NEGOTIATING WITH THE SOVIETS

The negotiation process extends to all phases of contacts with the Soviet side, including even social events. Western business representatives find their Soviet counterparts to be resourceful, relentless, well informed and well prepared. It would be wrong to suggest that there is any great mystery, any insuperable difficulty, or any specially evolved formulae for success in negotiating with the Soviets. They are very much like their Western counterparts: some are sophisticated, some are not; some are good-humored, some are not; some are clear and straightforward, some are not. While the style, pace and schedule of every negotiation is different, some general patterns have emerged.

Discussions typically begin about 9:00 AM, at the Soviet party's premises, around a conference table neatly arranged with bottles of mineral water and Pepsi-Cola, tea, coffee, cookies and cakes. Talks break for lunch around 1:00 PM. The midday meal can last till midafternoon; therefore, although talks may resume after lunch, they adjourn for the day not long thereafter.

As noted earlier, interpreters are usually supplied by the Soviet side, and they normally perform well. Russians tend toward unstructured discussions of commercial terms, and it is sometimes difficult to keep the talks focused on one point and to resolve it before moving on the next point. In the experience of some foreigners, Soviet negotiators talk a point to death. This may be an indication that they have yet to learn the truth of the adage that time is money. An apparent heedlessness at the amount of time consumed in unfocused discussion is particularly irksome, of course, to those who are in an alien setting, far from corporate headquarters, and usually eager to get home.

The draft documentation prepared by the foreign party is usually the point of departure for negotiations. The Soviets not only appear willing to work from texts you prepare, but are positively interested in learning from your drafts what ordinarily acceptable international contracts may contain. This disposition to work from your standard documentation affords some obvious advantages.

The Moscow Business Lunch. The parties often lunch together, with the restaurant and menu selected by the Soviet side. Such lunches are long, and the food heavy. The menu at the first such luncheon may seem wonderfully regal to the first-time visitor, but enthusiasm for the Moscow business lunch generally wanes when the foreign visitor realizes that the same fare — almost regardless of the restaurant — is served, with only marginal variations, at every single meal with Soviet negotiators. The meal typically begins with a course of cold appetizers: cold cuts including beef, pork, chicken, and beef tongue; various sausages; smoked fish, including sturgeon and sardines (both with bones); a cold salad of chopped or shredded carrots, peas and potatoes in mayonnaise dressing; and choice of an entree (invariably either very tough beefsteak or pork cutlet, breaded fish or chicken cutlet, or chicken Kiev) with roasted potatoes. Bowls of sour cream, mustard and butter accompany stacks of black, brown and white bread. The favorite dessert is ice cream with a sweet fruit or chocolate sauce. Beverages offered throughout the meal consist of mineral water, the ubiquitous Pepsi-Cola, an orange or lemon soft drink, Georgian wine, vodka, tea and coffee.

These feasts, which are punctuated by rounds of toasts, are not conducive to concluding negotiations in a timely fashion. In fact, don't expect to accomplish much in the way of negotiating after lunch. Mercifully, few evening meals are arranged by Soviet negotiators. Except for the few evenings spent at cultural events, you and other members of your negotiating team will find your evenings spent puzzling over drafts of documents to be discussed the following day, or trying to find a place for dinner outside of your hotel, or both. And whether you dine inside or outside your hotel, you will discover that evening meals very closely resemble the Moscow business lunch. Unfortunately, breakfast offers no relief: the next morning you will face many of the same foods, as well as sardines, pickled garlic cloves and beef tongue. Moscow's cuisine is not a dieter's nor a vegetarian's delight.

When asked how best to prepare for talks with Soviets, one experienced negotiator suggested that there could be no better advice than that contained in the Boy Scout Law, that is, to be "helpful, friendly, courteous, kind, obedient, cheerful, thrifty, brave, clean and reverent." While this may be useful general guidance, some particular problem areas are addressed in the section "Points for Joint Venture Negotiations."

THE AGREEMENT AND CHARTER

In this phase the parties refine the joint venture agreement and the charter, take steps to insure that the English and Russian language texts of the documents agree, and submit the documents for approval to the Ministry of Finance of the U.S.S.R.

The Appendix contains a checklist for a Joint Venture Agreement. Your agreement and charter will, of course, not completely conform to these checklists, but they should prove helpful to you in considering what provisions to include. You should also bear in mind that if your company has a standard agreement that it uses for certain kinds of business elsewhere in the world, such as for a joint venture in another country, you should not hesitate to ask your Soviet partner to accept your standard form as the basis for the text of your agreement in the U.S.S.R.

Finally, keep in mind that if a joint venture proves to be too complex a method for doing business with the Soviets, you may have a basis for a license agreement, or another kind of contract.

POINTS FOR JOINT VENTURE NEGOTIATIONS

Parties. Any legal entity, established and in good standing under the laws of a foreign jurisdiction, may become a party to a joint venture in the U.S.S.R. Sometimes, the foreign party first drawn to joint venture discussions in the Soviet Union decides in the course of negotiations that one of its subsidiaries or affiliates will be a more appropriate party to the joint venture. The Soviet side ordinarily has no problem with this, providing it is assured that the venture will receive the technology, experience or other performance possessed by the foreign parent company.

Under Soviet law, any legal entity may become a partner in a joint venture. This includes not only State enterprises, but cooperatives, institutes, factories and other kinds of organizations — as long as they have an independent legal personality. Individual persons may not become partners in joint ventures.

Scope and Purpose of the Venture. Realism should be both parties' guide when establishing the scope and purpose of the venture, either in protocols, the feasibility study or in the joint venture agreement itself. Goals that are stated in excessively broad, ambiguous or ambitious terms may cause the parties to deceive themselves about the benefits to be derived from their cooperative efforts. This sets the stage for disappointment and recrimination later.

The Joint Venture Is a Soviet Company. A joint venture established under the Soviet law is a Soviet legal entity. As such it is subject to all Soviet law except as otherwise provided in the joint venture legislation in the U.S.S.R. There are both benefits and burdens to this special status under Soviet law. One of the burdens, for example, is that the venture may be required to pay in hard currency for some goods and services obtained within the U.S.S.R., while a Soviet enterprise would be allowed to pay in rubles. Foreign personnel of a joint venture, based in the U.S.S.R., must pay hard currency for airline tickets and hotel rooms, while Soviet personnel may pay in rubles.

Limited Liability. Soviet law makes clear that an approved joint venture is entitled to limited liability. That is, like a corporation formed under U.S. law, the venture is liable on claims only to the extent of its assets, and the parties are liable only to the extent of their respective investments in the venture. The joint venture company is not liable for the debts or other liabilities of any of its constituent partners. Note, though, that there is as yet no legislation in the Soviet Union that details the attributes, rights and powers of a limited liability company. Therefore, all of the rights and powers of the enterprise are set forth in the Joint Venture Charter which, once approved, has the force of law. In this respect, a registered Soviet joint venture resembles the earliest kinds of English or Dutch joint stock companies whose powers were enumerated in a charter bestowed by the crown.

Ownership and Control. A foreign party may bo the majority shareholder in a Soviet joint venture, owning up to 99.9%. The joint venture law as originally drafted had capped the foreign share at a maximum of 49%. Unless otherwise agreed by the parties, of course, the capital contribution of the parties will determine their respective share ownership and control. Hence, if a foreign party wants a 90% share of the stock of the enterprise, and 90% control, it will be obligated to supply 90% of the invested capital. As a joint venture, of course, the enterprise requires at least two parties. Soviet law does not permit the establishment of a totally foreign-owned enterprise in the U.S.S.R.

The Authorized Fund. The investments, or contributions to capital, made by the parties create the authorized fund of the joint venture. These capital contributions can be made in the form of cash or other assets, or a combination of these. Contributions of the foreign party typically include hard currency cash, equipment, technology and know-how. The Soviet party's investment is normally made in the form of rubles, buildings, equipment and access to other resources. The authorized fund may be enlarged by additional contributions by the parties, or from the profits of the venture.

Valuation of Contributions to Capital. Contributions to capital may be valued in foreign currency, in rubles, or both. Putting a value on the respective contributions of the parties is ordinarily one of the most difficult stages of the joint venture negotiations. Unlike the ruble, the dollar is, of course, freely convertible on international exchange markets and has an established value; but sometimes — where the Soviet side is making its investment in rubles — maddening differences can arise over the relative value of the dollar to the ruble.

This valuation problem is not confined to the nonconvertibility of the ruble. It extends also to technology and equipment. Setting a value on equipment, for example, for which a recognized world market price exists and is readily ascertainable poses no problem. However, when no such reference price is available (such as on special equipment that is proprietary to one of the parties, or where proprietary technology and know-how are involved), valuation is left to often arduous negotiation. The same holds true for factory buildings contributed by the Soviet side; there has been a tendency, from the point of view of foreign investors, to very considerable overvaluation by Soviet parties.

A foreign party should be thoroughly prepared to explain and defend the value it attaches to machinery, equipment or technology it proposes to invest as its non-cash share in the authorized fund. It should also be prepared to closely examine the values attached to buildings, equipment and technology that the Soviet side proposes to invest. One troubling aspect of the overvaluation of the buildings that form part of the Soviet party's investment is that the value of such facilities lies in the fact that they are scarce in the U.S.S.R. The same facilities would be of far less value outside the U.S.S.R.

Tax Planning. A potential U.S. investor in a Soviet joint venture should take utmost care in its tax planning, insofar as both U.S. and Soviet taxes are concerned. Although there is a U.S.-Soviet tax treaty in effect, it dates from more than a decade ago and will likely be replaced in 1990 by a new treaty. The terms of the new treaty will be important for prospective joint venturers (e.g., provisions reducing the rate of witholding taxes imposed by the U.S.S.R.). It should also be noted that U.S. tax law contains provisions that may make it more desirable for a U.S. party to license its technology to the joint venture, rather than contribute it as capital to the authorized fund. These provisions could result in unexpected U.S. excise or "deemed royalty" taxes on contributed technology.

Soviet law imposes a tax of 30% on joint venture profits, and a further 20% witholding tax on the foreign repatriation of after-tax profits. However, certain tax incentives are available. Joint ventures are entitled to a holiday from income tax for the first two years in which the venture realizes a profit. This tax holiday period is three years for ventures that are located in the Far East Economic Region of the U.S.S.R. Depending on when a profit is declared, the actual period of tax exemption can extend beyond two or three years. Under certain conditions, such as if the joint venture affords unique benefits to the Soviet Union, the Ministry of Finance may be persuaded to approve longer periods of tax exemption.

Determining the joint venture tax due involves applying certain deductions to gross income. The first category of deductions covers revenues devoted to the creation of a Reserve Fund, and a Fund for the Development of Production, Science and Technology. While these funds are mandated by law, no specific time is established within which the funds must be fully funded. The reserve fund must become 25% of the authorized fund. A second category of deductions is the more familiar itemization of business expenses incurred. Depreciation is allowed in the computation of deductions, on the straight-line method based on asset cost.

Soviet Customs Duties. Equipment, materials and other property imported into the U.S.S.R. as part of a foreign party's contribution to the authorized fund is exempt from Soviet customs duties. Reduction or exemption of Soviet customs duties is also available on goods imported into the U.S.S.R. for the needs of the joint venture's development or production.

Foreign Exchange Problems. Generally speaking, a joint venture is expected to meet all of its foreign exchange expenses from its foreign exchange earnings. This means, among other things, that if the foreign party expects to receive its profits or royalty payments in hard currency, the venture must earn hard currency. It also means that hard currency must be available for the purchase of any raw materials or equipment that must be obtained from abroad, or for the payment of principal and interest of foreign loans. Lately, the Soviet partners in joint ventures have sought to receive at least part of their profits in foreign exchange.

Export of goods and services is generally the only way in which a venture can earn foreign exchange, although it is true that some Soviet enterprises have hard currency with which to pay for the venture's goods and services sold on the domestic market. The Soviet government does not provide the foreign joint venture party with guarantees that any portion of the rubles earned from domestic sales will be convertible into foreign exchange, nor, despite experimentation with currency auctions, are there other effective measures available for the conversion of rubles to foreign exchange.

Such transactions as barter or countertrade have been attempted, with marginal success, to overcome the problems posed by the nonconvertible ruble. Presented with the accumlated-ruble dilemma — and perhaps inspired by the success enjoyed by PepsiCo, Inc., in financing its expansion in the U.S.S.R. by swapping Pepsi concentrate for Stolichnaya vodka — some foreign investors reason that if their joint venture accumulates rubles from sales on the Soviet domestic market, they will be able to utilize those rubles to purchase needed Soviet raw materials, or purchase Soviet commodities that can be resold for hard currency outside the U.S.S.R. The problem with this approach is that it works in theory but not in practice. Why should a Soviet enterprise that has commodities available for a hard-currency market sell those commodities for rubles? The difficulty with this approach was compounded by Soviet legislation issued in 1989 that permits joint ventures to export only their own products, and import only products to meet their own needs.

Pricing, Marketing and Quality Control. In most instances, a fundamental purpose of a joint enterprise involving Soviet and foreign parties is to enhance the acceptability of Soviet goods — in the U.S.S.R. and abroad. It is fair to say that with few exceptions, Soviet goods have been priced without regard to real costs of production, that they are notorious for inferior quality, and that marketing and channels of distribution have become monsters of inefficiency, suffocated by bureaucracy. The close collaboration possible in the joint venture form of doing business affords a remedy to these ills, but only to the extent that the foreign and Soviet parties can realistically and effectively work together. The foreign party may find itself, outside the framework of negotiating a joint venture agreement, conducting technical seminars and training sessions for the Soviet side on these subjects.

Training. The foreign joint venture partner may also become responsible for training Soviet management and technical personnel outside the U.S.S.R. The joint venture agreement should be very precise as to the scope and extent of such training, the number and selection of trainees, and the allocation of cost for training.

Management of the Venture. Two levels of management are contemplated by Soviet joint venture legislation: a Board of Directors and a Directorate.

The Board of Directors is composed of persons selected by each party, normally in proportion to the party's respective share in the authorized fund. By law, all fundamental decisions are to be decided unanimously by the Board. The Charter ordinarily lists or describes what kinds of decisions require unanimous agreement. Typically the Board meets periodically during the year, perhaps twice. A foreigner may be named Chairman of the Board.

The Directorate consists of a General Director, a Deputy General Director, and such other directors as may be necessary for the day-to-day management of the enterprise. The functions of these managers are normally spelled out in the joint venture agreement or the charter.

Labor Relations. A joint venture is allowed a great deal of flexibility in its labor-management relations. The rights to hire and fire personnel, set levels of compensation, and provide for incentives, for example, are granted. But foreign investors should keep in mind that Soviet law mandates that joint venture employees must consist mainly of Soviet personnel and that a collective labor agreement consistent with Soviet labor law must be concluded between management and a trade union organization with respect to the conditions of employment for those workers. Payment of salaries and incentives to Soviet workers must be in the form of rubles, not convertible currency, though there is apparently no prohibition against incentives in the form of highly-prized foreign consumer goods.

The venture may also employ foreign workers. The terms of their employment are generally set by personal services contracts. Foreign workers are subject to personal income tax in the U.S.S.R., but they are also entitled to certain benefits with respect to taxation, customs duties on personal items and repatriation of after-tax salary in convertible currency.

Accounting and Auditing. As in any business, joint ventures require detailed financial record keeping. There are variances between the accounting principles and methods employed in the U.S.S.R. and those generally accepted accounting principles with which U.S. firms are more familiar. This must be kept in mind when establishing an accounting system for the venture. Accounting in the U.S.S.R. is generally done on the cash, rather than the accrual, method. The fiscal year is normally the calendar year.

Soviet law requires that a Soviet legal entity, such as A/O Inaudit, perform the audit function. Some of the large international accounting firms have established joint ventures with Soviet entities, and those entities are also authorized to perform the audit function. A foreign party in a joint venture may, at its own expense, have an independent audit conducted by the foreign firm of its choice.

Approval and Registration. Once the feasibility study, the joint venture agreement and the charter have been negotiated, they must be submitted for review and approval by the Ministry of Finance of the U.S.S.R., or another appropriate authority acting with the authority of the Finance Ministry. Once approval has been given, the enterprise receives a certificate of registration. The documents submitted, sometimes referred to as "the Foundation Documents," must then be presented to the Department of State Revenue of the Ministry of Finance.

Language. Where U.S. companies are concerned, the joint venture agreement and the charter are normally negotiated on the basis of an English language text. However, the final agreements are invariably executed in two texts, English and Russian. A provision is typically included which states that the two texts are "equally authentic." It is the Russian text which is approved by the authorities in the registration process. It is obviously essential for both sides to take every reasonable step, utilizing the services of competent, independent translators familiar with "legalese," to assure that the English and Russian texts are in all material respects identical. Disputes of some degree are inevitable in all business ventures, and they may be particularly intractible when it turns out they are caused by manifest contradictions in the English and Russian texts of the agreement or charter.

VII

SOVIET LAWS

TRADEMARKS

Soviet law provides for the registration and protection
of trademarks, including foreign trademarks, under the
Trademark Statute of 1974, as amended. Trademarks
are registered at the State Committee on Inventions and
Discoveries of the Council of Ministers of the U.S.S.R. A
foreigner generally makes application for the registration of a trademark to the Patent Bureau of the U.S.S.R.
Chamber of Commerce and Industry, through an organization known as Soyuzpatent, which functions as the
agent of the foreign applicant.

On application forms provided by Soyuzpatent, the
foreign applicant must provide its legal name, address,
nationality and proposes use of the trademark, together
with 25 copies of the trademark, a list of goods or services with which it proposes to use the trademark, and a
power of attorney to Soyuzpatent to enable it to fulfill the
formalities of application. If priority is claimed under the
Paris Convention, the application must also contain a
certified copy of the foreign certificate (or application).

Action on foreign trademark applications must be
made within six months. A certificate is issued if the
application is approved. If the application is denied, the
applicant has a right to appeal. Trademarks may be the
subject of license or assignment agreements.

Trademark protection is available for ten years, renewable for additional terms. Once registered, the trademark must be used within five years or it is subject to cancellation or compulsory licensing. In the event of infringement, the trademark owner may seek to enjoin the unauthorized use, bring a civil suit for damages, and institute action for criminal sanctions under the criminal codes of the various republics.

The Soviet Union became a signatory to the Paris Convention for the Protection of Industrial Property in 1965, and a signatory to the Madrid Agreement for the International Registration of Trademarks in 1976.

COPYRIGHTS

As of 1973, the Soviet Union is a signatory to the Universal Copyright Convention (UCC). Foreigners as well as Soviet citizens can obtain copyright protection in the U.S.S.R. Protection of an author's copyrighted material extends for the author's lifetime plus 25 years from January 1st of the year following the author's death. Soviet law provides that copyright protection is effective upon publication. Protection accorded to foreign copyright holders may depend on when and where the work was first published abroad. Soviet law recognizes a translator's right to obtain a copyright on his or her translation of another's work, providing the translation was done with the author's permission. Foreign parties seeking general information about copyright protection, or wishing to publish works in the Soviet Union, should contact:

Copyright Agency of the U.S.S.R. (VAAP)
B. Bronnaya 6A
Moscow K-104
103670
Tel.: 203-4405 or 203-5551
Fax: 200-1263
Telex: 411327 (ATVR)

PATENTS

Protection of inventions and discoveries in the U.S.S.R. is governed by the 1973 Statute on Discoveries, Inventions and Rationalization Proposals of the Council of Ministers of the U.S.S.R., as amended in 1978, and various other agreements to which the Soviet Union is a party. Beginning in 1965, the U.S.S.R. has adhered to the Paris Convention for the Protection of Industrial Property, and in 1977 the U.S.S.R. ratified the 1970 Convention on Patent Cooperation.

As with trademarks, a foreign patent holder may apply for patent protection in the Soviet Union. Applications are made to Patent Bureau of the U.S.S.R. Chamber of Commerce and Industry in Moscow, which for a fee and pursuant to a power of attorney, functions as agent of the foreign applicant. Protection against patent infringement is available by way of a civil court action for damages to establish royalties due and injunctive action to enjoin the infringement.

A foreign patent-owner may license the patent's use on commercial terms customary in international practice. Licensees in the Soviet Union have in the past preferred to make lump-sum payments under a license rather than royalty payments tied to inputs or to units of production. Recently, royalties have increasingly become an acceptable basis for payment to foreign patent holders under a license.

REPRESENTATIVE OFFICES IN MOSCOW

Under regulations promulgated in November 1989, foreign companies may apply for approval to establish a resident representative office in Moscow, through an accreditation process. Practical benefits from accredited office status include the privilege of assigning foreign personnel to Moscow; maintenance of an office from which contacts can be maintained with Soviet customers, suppliers or business partners; employment of Soviet nationals; and ownership of motor vehicles. Accreditation also entitles the office to obtain such necessary support facilities as telex and telephone links and housing for expatriate personnel.

These and other benefits are available to joint ventures, of course, but they are not available to unaccredited business representatives sojourning in Moscow. Control over foreigners, and over the scarce supplies of office space and apartments, is managed through a Soviet government organization, the Service Administration for the Diplomatic Corps (UPDK). Accredited companies must apply to UPDK for much of what they want in Moscow, because it is not possible to make private arrangements for such provisions as rental of office premises, lease of apartments, and installation of communications facilities. Because of the high cost of office space and apartments, and the salary and associated costs needed to support expatriates in Moscow, it is mostly larger companies that have established accredited offices in Moscow.

Foreign companies wishing to establish an accredited Moscow office must, as a first step, secure the assistance of a Soviet sponsoring organization. Normally, the sponsor is a Soviet trade organization which has established a sound commercial relationship over a period of time with the applicant. Consideration of applications can take time, sometimes up to two years. Once established, the accredited office is a taxable entity, and its foreign personnel who reside in Moscow are subject to Soviet income taxation.

VIII

U.S. EXPORT CONTROL REGULATIONS

EXPORT CONTROLS

The United States employs a number of export control laws that restrict the export of various commodities to other countries. These export control laws were enacted for four reasons: national security; foreign policy considerations; nuclear nonproliferation; and protection of the economy from reductions in scarce resources.

The centerpiece of the U.S. program of export control is the Export Administration Act and the Export Administration Regulations (the Regulations) promulgated thereunder. The Department of Commerce, Bureau of Export Administration (BXA), enforces the Regulations to ensure compliance with U.S. export controls. These Regulations contain information on obtaining an export license, documentation requirements, special nuclear controls, re-exports, technical data, special commodity and country policies, and other essential guidance on exporting.

The Regulations also include the Commodity Control List under which almost every commodity exported from the U.S. may be classified. This list explains the Commerce Department's level of control on certain commodities for export to certain destinations and identifies, among other things, countries for which a validated export license is required to export each commodity, the reason the commodity is controlled, and any special licenses that may be available for exporting that commodity.

Exporters should remember that violations of the Export Administration Regulations carry both civil and criminal penalties, so if in doubt, U.S. Department of Commerce officials or qualified professional consultants should be contacted for assistance in complying with export regulations.

EXPORT LICENSING

United States Export Control laws are enforced primarily through the licensing of export commodities. The export of all goods and technology is licensed through two types of export licenses: general and validated.

A General License. This is a broad grant of authority by the government to all exporters for certain categories of products to all or most destinations. Most U.S. exports are shipped abroad under general licenses, and no application is required for their use. There are about 21 different types of general licenses.

A Validated License. This is a specific grant of authority from the government to a particular exporter to export a particular product to a certain destination. Licenses are granted on a case-by-case basis for a single transaction and generally are valid for two years. Certain special licenses are also available to cover a range of products to several distributors. The most well-known of these is the Distribution License. An exporter must apply to Commerce's Office of Export Licensing for a validated export license.

Licensing Procedures. Except for U.S. territories and possessions and, in most cases, Canada, most items exported require either a general or validated export license. Several agencies of the U.S. government are involved in the license review process.

The first step in the export licensing process is to determine whether a product requires a general or a validated license. This depends on what is being exported, where it is going, the end use and the end user. Basically, this is a three-step procedure:

1. The destination of the product—A firm must check the Country Groups schedule contained in the Regulations to see which category the export destination falls under.

2. Commodity exported—The firm must check the Commodity Control List to see whether the product requires a validated license for shipment to the Country Groups identified in the preceding step.

3. Finally, the firm must determine whether any special restrictions apply to the export transaction.

An exporter probably will have to apply for a validated export license if the export is:

- A strategic commodity—One that is capable of contributing significantly to the military potential of any adversary of the U.S.

- A short-supply commodity—One that is limited in the U.S. If it were to be exported without restriction, there would be an excessive drain on U.S. supplies and a serious inflationary impact on the U.S. economy. This control, however, is rarely applied.

- Any other commodity to a destination where there are foreign policy concerns.

- Unpublished technical data—This refers to technical information (generally related to the design, production or use of a product) that is not available to the public. It is not described in detail in books, magazines or pamphlets, nor is it taught in colleges or universities. It is information that a person will not release without charging for it.

If you need to obtain a validated export license, you must fill out an application (form ITA-622P). The application is complex, and you should be careful when completing it. A guide, "The Export License: How to Fill Out the Application," is available from your district office of the Investment Trade Administration (ITA) or from the BXA.

ADDITIONAL DOCUMENTATION

In addition to filing an application for a validated license, certain applications must be supported by documents supplied by the prospective purchaser or the government of the country of destination. By reviewing the Regulations, the exporter can determine whether any supporting documents are required.

For example, the "International Import Certificate" is a statement issued by the government of the country of destination that certifies that the exported products will be disposed of responsibly in the designated country. The "Statement of Ultimate Consignee and Purchaser" (Form BXA-629P) is written assurance that the foreign purchaser of the goods will not resell or dispose of the goods in a manner contrary to the export license under which the goods were originally exported.

In addition to obtaining the appropriate export license, U.S. exporters should be careful to inquire about all other international trade regulations established by specific legislation or other authority of the U.S government, such as regulations under the International Traffic in Arms Regulations, the Office of Foreign Assets Control or relevant anti-boycott restrictions. Also, the exporter should keep in mind that the import regulations of foreign countries must also be met. It should be noted that the exporter bears the ultimate responsibility for the accuracy of all statements made on the relevant licenses and export documentation.

POINTS OF INTEREST FOR EXPORTERS

The following information will be of use to U.S. exporters. **Government Agencies.** BXA's major offices involved in administering export controls include:

- Office of Export Licensing

- Office of Technology and Policy Analysis

- Office of Foreign Availability

Normal Processing times. The average export license processing times are:

- Applications to COCOM member countries—5 days; 40% fall into this category.

- Applications with no referral to an outside agency—10 days; 40%.

- Applications that are referred for interagency review and COCOM—120 days; 2%.

- Applications that are referred for interagency review (not COCOM)—50 days; 18%.

RUSSIAN
LANGUAGE
GUIDE

The following vocabulary section is by no means exhaustive, and is intended to provide only the most rudimentary tools for communicating in Russian. It is far beyond the scope of this guide to explain such complexities of the Russian language as palatalization and gender endings. When using this guide, also remember that, like English, Russian is not a phonetic language. Therefore, pronunciation of combinations of letters can differ from those letter's individual pronunciations. Finally, the English transcriptions that follow contain italicized syllables, which indicate those syllables that should be stressed.

While it is true that travelers using this language guide may never be mistaken for natives, they hopefully will be able to get what they want and go where they want by using it.

THE CYRILLIC ALPHABET

PRINTED LETTERS	ENGLISH PHONETIC TRANSCRIPTION
Аа	ah, uh
Бб	b
Вв	v, f
Гг	g
Дд	d
Ее	eh, yeh, ih
Жж	jh, zh
Зз	z
Ии	ih, ee
Йй	yuh
Кк	k
Лл	l
Мм	m
Нн	n
Оо	uh, aw
Пп	p
Рр	r
Сс	s
Тт	t
Уу	oo
Фф	f
Хх	kh
Цц	ts
Чч	ch
Шш	sh
Щщ	shch
Ъъ	no sound
Ыы	ih
Ьь	soft sign*
Ээ	eh
Юю	yoo
Яя	yah

*The soft sign softens the last consonant of the word.

NUMBERS

ENGLISH	RUSSIAN	ENGLISH PHONETIC TRANSCRIPTION
one	ОДИН	uh-*deen*
two	ДВА	dvah
three	ТРИ	tree
four	ЧЕТЫРЕ	chi-*ty*-reh
five	ПЯТЬ	pyaht
six	ШЕСТЬ	shehst
seven	СЕМЬ	sehm
eight	ВОСЕМЬ	*vaw*-sim
nine	ДЕВЯТЬ	*deh*-vuht
ten	ДЕСЯТЬ	*deh*-suht
eleven	ОДИННАДЦАТЬ	uh *deen*-nuh-tsuht
twelve	ДВЕНАДЦАТЬ	dvi-*nah*-tsuht
thirteen	ТРИНАДЦАТЬ	tri-*nuh*-tsuht
fourteen	ЧЕТЫРНАДЦАТЬ	chi-*tyr*-nuh-tsuht
fifteen	ПЯТНАДЦАТЬ	pyaht-*nah*-tsuht
sixteen	ШЕСТНАДЦАТЬ	shyst-*nah*-tsuht
seventeen	СЕМНАДЦАТЬ	sim-*nah*-tsuht
eighteen	ВОСЕМНАДЦАТЬ	vuh-sim-*nah*-tsuht
nineteen	ДЕВЯТНАДЦАТЬ	di-vuht-*nah*-tsuht
twenty	ДВАДЦАТЬ	*dvah*-tsuht
twenty-one	ДВАДЦАТЬ ОДИН	*dvah*-tsuht uh-*deen*
twenty-two	ДВАДЦАТЬ ДВА	*dvah*-tsuht dvah
twenty-three	ДВАДЦАТЬ ТРИ	*dvah*-tsuht tree
thirty	ТРИДЦАТЬ	*tree*-tsuht
forty	СОРОК	*saw*-ruhk
fifty	ПЯТЬДЕСЯТ	pyaht-di-*saht*
sixty	ШЕСТЬДЕСЯТ	shyst-di-*saht*
seventy	СЕМЬДЕСЯТ	*sehm*-di-suht
eighty	ВОСЕМЬДЕСЯТ	*vaw*-sim-di-suht
ninety	ДЕВЯНОСТО	deh-vuh-*naws*-tuh
one hundred	СТО	staw
two hundred	ДВЕСТИ	*dvehs*-ti
three hundred	ТРИСТА	*trees*-tuh
four hundred	ЧЕТЫРЕСТА	chi-*ty*-ris-tuh
five hundred	ПЯТЬСОТ	pyaht-*sawt*
six hundred	ШЕСТЬСОТ	shyst-*sawt*
one thousand	ТЫСЯЧА	*ty*-suh-chuh
five thousand	ПЯТЬ ТЫСЯЧ	paht *ty*-suhch

ENGLISH	RUSSIAN
Yes.	Да.
No.	Нет.
Please.	Пожалуйста.
Thank you.	Спасибо.
You're welcome.	Пожалуйста.
Hello!	Здравствуйте!
Good morning!	Доброе утро!
Good evening!	Добрый вечер!
Good night!	Спокойной ночи!
Good-bye!	До свидания!
Good luck!	Всего хорошего!
How are you?	Как вы поживаете?
Fine, thank you.	Спасибо, хорошо.
Excuse me.	Извините меня.
My name is...	Меня зовут...
Pleased to meet you!	Очень приятно!
Do you speak...?	Вы говорите...?
I do (not) speak...	Я (не) говорю...
Russian	по-русски
English	по-английски
French	по-французски
German	по-немецки
I read (a little)...	Я (немного) читаю...
Speak slowly.	Говорите помедленнее.
I do (not) understand.	Я (не) понимаю.
Please repeat.	Повторите, пожалуйста.
Write it down.	Напишите это.
I (we) need a translator.	Мне (нам) нужен переводчик.
Tell me.	Скажите мне.
Show me.	Покажите мне.
Give me.	Дайте мне.
Bring me.	Принесите мне.
Help me.	Помогите мне.
I do (not)...	Я (не)...
know	знаю
want	хочу
I do (not) need...	Мне (не) нужно...
Do you...?	Вы ...?
know	знаете
want	хотите
Do you need...	Вам нужно?
Where?	Где?
When?	Когда?
Who?	Кто?
Why?	Почему?
What?	Что?
How?	Как?

ENGLISH PHONETIC TRANSCRIPTION

Dah.
Nyeht.
Puh-*jhahl*-stuh.
Spuh-*see*-buh.
Puh-*jhahl*-stuh.
Zdrahv-stvooy-teh!

Daw-brah-yeh *oo*-truh!
Daw bry *veh*-chir!
Spuh *koi*-noi *naw*-chi!
Duh svi-*dah*-nyuh!
Vcee-vuh khuh-*ruh*-sheh-vuh!

Kahk vy puh-jhen-*vah*-yet-eh?
Spuh-*see*-buh, khuh-ruh-*shaw*.
Iz-vin-*eet*-eh mehn-*yah*.

Mehn-*yah* zah-*voot*...
Aw-chin pri-*yaht* nuh puhz-nah-*kuhm*-eets yah!
Vy gahv-ah-*reet*-eh...?
Yah (nyeh) gahv-ahr-*yoo*...
  puh-*roo*-skee
  puh-ahn-*glee*-skee
  puh-frahn-*tsoo*-skee
  puh-nim-*yeht*-skee
Yah (nim-*naw*-guh-vuh) chi-*tah*-yoo...
Gahv-ah-*reet*-eh puh-*mehd* lin-eh-yeh.
Yah (nyeh) puh ni-*mah*-yoo.
Puhv-tuh-*ree*-teh, puh-*jhahl*-stuh.
Zah-pi-*shee*-teh *eh*-tuh.
Mehn-*yeh* (nahm) *noo*-jhehn pi-ri-*vuhd*-chik.

Skah-*jhee*-teh mehn-*yeh*.
Puh-kuh-*jhy*-teh mehn-*yeh*.
Dah-*eet*-eh mehn-*yeh*.
Pri-ni-*seet*-eh mehn-*yeh*.
Puh-maw-*geet*-eh mehn-*yeh*.

Yah (nyeh)...
  znah-yoo
  khuh-*choo*
Mehn-*yeh* (nyeh) *noojh*-nuh...
Vy...?
  znah-yeet-eh
  khuh-*teet*-eh
Vahm *noojh*-nah...?

Gdeh?
Kuhg-*dah*?
Ktaw?
Puh-chi-*moo*?
Shtaw?
Kahk?

ENGLISH	RUSSIAN
What time is it?	Который час?
Tomorrow	Завтра
Yesterday	Вчера
Last night	Вчера вечером
It's warm.	Тепло.
It's cold.	Холодно.
It's raining (snowing).	Идет дождь (снег).
I feel warm.	Мне тепло.
I feel cold.	Мне холодно.
I am tired.	Я устал.

DAYS OF THE WEEK

Monday	Понедельник
Tuesday	Вторник
Wednesday	Среда
Thursday	Четверг
Friday	Пятница
Saturday	Суббота
Sunday	Воскресенье

PUBLIC SIGNS

Entrance (forbidden)	Вход (Входа нет)
Exit (forbidden)	Выход (Выхода нет)
Crossing (forbidden)	Переход (Перехода нет)
Stop	Стойте
Go	Идите
Men's room	Мужской туалет
Women's room	Женский туалет

AIRPORT AND CUSTOMS

General

Airport	Аэропорт
Information bureau	Справочное бюро
Flight (number)	Рейс (номер)
Arrival	Прилет
Departure	Отлет
Boarding gate	Выход на посадку
When does the flight leave for...?	Когда отправляется самолет на...?
When does the flight arrive in...?	Когда самолет прибывает в...?
Is there a bus connection to...?	Есть ли автобус до...?
the city center	центра города
the hotel	гостиницы
How much luggage may I take?	Сколько багажа разрешается взять?

BAGGAGE

Baggage pick-up area	Выдача багажа
Baggage check-in	Багажная квитанция
I want my luggage.	Я хочу взять свой багаж.
I lost my luggage.	Я потерял свой багаж.
I need a porter.	Мне нужен носильщик.

ENGLISH PHONETIC TRANSCRIPTION

Kuh-*taw*-ry chahs.
Zahf-truh
Fchi-*rah*
Fchi-*rah veh*-chi-ruhm

Teh-pluh.
Khaw-luhd-nuh.
Ee-*dawt* dawzhd (snehk).
Mehn-*yeh teh*-pluh.
Mehn-*yeh khaw*-luhd-nuh.
Yah oos-*tahl*.

Puh-ni-*dehl*-nik
Ftawr-nik
Sri-*dah*
Chit-*vehrk*
Paht-ni-tsuh
Soob-*baw*-tuh
Vuh-skri-*seh*-neh

Vkhawd *(vkhuw*-duh nyeht)
Vy-khuhd *(vy*-khuh-dud nyeht)
Pi-ri-*khuht* (pi-ri-*khuh*-duh nyeht)
Stoi-*eet*-eh
I-*deet*-eh
Moojh-skoi too-uh-*leht*
Jhehn-skee too-uh-*leht*

Uh-eh-ruh-*pawrt*
Sprah-vuhch-nuh-yeh boo-*raw*
Reh-*ees* (*naw*-mir)
Pri-*lyuht*
Uht-*leht*
Vy-khuht na *puh*-suhd-koo
Kuhg-*dah* uht-prahv-*lyah*-
    ehts-yah suh-muh-*lawt* nah...?
Kuhg-*dah* pri-hy-*vah*-yet
    suh-muh-*lawt* v...?
Ehst lee uhf-*taw*-boos duh...?
    tsehn-troo *gaw*-ruh-duh
    guhs-*tee*-ni-tseh
Skawl-kuh buh-*gahsh*-ah
    rahz-reh-*shah*-yehts yah
    vzyaht?

Vy-duh-chah buh-*gahsh* ah
Buh-*gahsh*-nah-yah kvi-*tahn*-tsee-yah
Yah khuh-*choo* vzyaht svoi buh-*gahsh*.
Yah puh-ti-*rahl* svoi buh-*gahsh*.
Mehn-*yeh noo*-jhehn nuh-*seel*-shchik.

ENGLISH	RUSSIAN

CUSTOMS

Customs	Таможня
Here is...	Вот...
my luggage	мой багаж
my passport	мой паспорт
my visa	моя виза
Must I open everything?	Должен ли я все открывать?
There are only...in here.	Здесь только...
clothes	одежда
books	книги
gifts	подарки
This is all I have.	Это все, что у меня есть.
Is that all?	Это все?

TRANSPORTATION

General travel

Intourist office	Бюро Интуриста
Show me the way to...	Покажите мне дорогу к...
Show me on the map.	Покажите мне на карте.
I am lost.	Я заблудился.
How long does it take to get to...?	Сколько времени, чтобы доехать...?

Driving a car

Car	Машина
I have a license.	У меня есть права.
Where is the road to...?	Как проехать к...?
Where does this road go?	Куда ведет эта дорога?
Gas station	Бензоколонка
Garage	Гараж
Gasoline	Бензин
How much per liter?	Сколько стоит литр бензина?
Give me. . .liters.	Дайте, пожалуйста, ...литров.
Do you have a road map?	У вас есть дорожная карта?
My car has broken down.	Моя машина сломалась.
Can you...?	Можете ли вы...?
push me	подтолкнуть меня

Taxis

Taxi	Такси
Please call a taxi for me.	Пожалуйста, вызовите мне такси.
I want to go to...	Мне нужно проехать к...
How far is it?	Как далеко это?
Far	Далеко
Not far	Недалеко
How much will it cost?	Сколько это будет стоить?
Please drive...	Поезжайте, пожалуйста...
more carefully	осторожнее
more slowly	медленнее
faster	быстрее
Stop here; I want to get out.	Остановитесь здесь; я хочу выйти.
Please wait for me.	Подождите меня, пожалуйста.
How much do I owe you?	Сколько я вам должен?
Keep the change.	Сдачи не надо.

ENGLISH PHONETIC TRANSCRIPTION

Tah-*mawjh*-nah-yah
Vuht...
  moi buh-*gahsh*
  moi *pahs*-puhrt
  moi-*yah* vee-zuh
Duhl-jhehn lee yah vsoi uht-*kry*-vaht?
Zdehs *tuhl*-kuh...
  uh-*dehjh*-duh
  knee-gee
  puh-*dahr*-kee
Uh-tuh vseh shtaw ou mehn-*yuh* yest.
Eh-tuh vsaw?

Boo-*raw* Ehn-too-*rees*-tuh
Puh-kuh-*jhy*-teh mehn-*yeh* duh-ruh-gook...
Puh-kuh-*jhy*-teh mehn-*yeh* nah *kahrt*-eh.
Yah zuh-bloo-*deel*-suh.
Skawl kuh *vreh* mi ni, *ohtaw* by duh *yeh* khaht...?

Muh-*shy*-nuh
Oo mehn-*yah* yehst prah-*vah*.
Kahk pruh-*yeh*-khaht k...?
Kuh-*dah* veh-*dyot* eh-tuh duh-*ruh*-gah?
Behn-zah-*kawl*-ahn-kah
Guh-*rahsh*
Behn-*zeen*
Skawl-kuh *staw*-yit *lee*-tr behn-*zee*-nuh?
Deye-teh puh-*jhahl*-stuh . . . lee-truhv.
Oo vahs yehst duh-*rawjh*-nuh-yuh-*kahr*-tuh
Muh-*yah* muh-*shy*-nuh slaw-*muhl*-ahs.
Maw-jhy-teh li vy...?
  puhd-tuhlk-*noot* mehn-*yah*

Tuhk-*see*
Puh-*jhahl*-stuh, *vi*-zuh-veet-eh mehn-*yeh* tuhk-*see*.
Mehn-*yah* dahl-eh-kuh *noojh*-naw pruh-*yeh*-khaht k...
Kahk *dahl*-eh-kuh eh-tuh?
Dahl-eh-kuh
Nyeh-*dahl*-eh-kuh
Skawl-kuh eh-tuh *boo*-dit *staw*-yit?
Puh-*jhahl*-stuh, puh-yiz-*jheye*-teh...
  uhs-tuh-*rawjh*-nih-yeh
  mehd-lin-ni-yeh
  bis-*treh*-yeh
Uhs-tuh-nuh-*vee*-tis zdehs; yah khuh-*choo uy*-tee
Puh-duhjh-*dee*-teh mehn-*yah*, puh-*jhahl*-stuh.
Skawl-kuh yah vahm *duhl*-jhehn?
Sdah-chi nyeh *nah*-duh.

ENGLISH	RUSSIAN

Bus, trolley and metro

Bus	Автобус
Bus stop	Остановка автобуса
Trolley	Троллейбус
Trolley stop	Остановка троллейбуса
Metro (subway)	Метро
Metro station	Станция метро
Which (bus, trolley, metro) goes to...?	Какой (автобус, троллейбус, поезд метро) идет до...
How much is the fare?	Сколько стоит проезд?
Do I have to transfer	Нужна ли пересадка?
Please tell me where to get off.	Скажите мне, пожалуйста, где сойти.

Trains

Train	Поезд
Station	Вокзал
Ticket office	Билетная касса
Waiting room	Зал ожидания
When?	Когда?
From which platform?	С какой платформы?
From which station...? does the train leave for...?	С какого вокзала отправляется поезд до...?
Is the train arriving...? on time late	Поезд прибывает...? вовремя с опозданием
Is this seat taken?	Это место занято.

AT THE HOTEL

Service bureau	Бюро обслуживания
Floor Supervisor	Горничная
I have a reservation for... tonight three days one person two people	У меня заказан номер на... сегодняшнюю ночь три дня одного человека двух человек
What is the rate per...? day week	Сколько стоит номер на...? один день неделю
I would like to speak to the manager.	Я бы хотел поговорить с администратором.
My room key, please.	Ключ от моего номера, пожалуйста.
Don't disturb me before...	Не беспокойте меня до...
I am leaving at... o' clock a.m.	Я уезжаю в...часов утра.
Please prepare my bill.	Подготовьте, пожалуйста, счет.

COMMUNICATIONS
Telephone and telegram

Telephone	Телефон
Where is a telephone booth?	Где телефон-автомат?
Will you telephone for me?	Позвоните, пожалуйста, за меня.
Will you send a telegram for me?	Пошлите, пожалуйста, за меня телеграмму.

ENGLISH PHONETIC TRANSCRIPTION

Uhv-*taw*-boos
Uhs-tuh-*nawv*-kuh uhv-*taw*-boo-suh
Truh-lee-*boos*
Uhs-tuh-*nawv*-kuh truh-*lee*-boos-ah
Mit-*ruh*
Stahn-tsi-yuh mit-*ruh*
Kah-*koi* (uhv-*taw*-boos, truh-lee-*boos*, mit-*ruh*) i-*dyuht* duh...?

Skawl-kuh *staw*-yit pruh-*yehzd?*
Noojh-nuh li pehr-eh-*sahd*-kah?
Skuh-*jhy*-teh mehn-*yeh* puh-*jhahl*-stuh,
   gdeh soi-yee-*teh*.

Paw-yehzd
Vuhg-*zahl*
Bi-*leht*-nuh-yuh *kahs*-suh
Zahl awjh-ih-*dahn*-ih-yah
Kuhg-*dah?*
Skah-*kvi* pluht-*fawr*-my?
Skuh-*kaw*-vuh vuhg-*zah*-luh...
   uht-*prahv*-lyah-ehts-yah *paw*-yehzt duh...?
Paw-yehzd prih-bee-*vah*-yeht...?
   vaw-vreh-myah
   cuh-*puhz*-dah-neh-yeht
Eh-tuh *mehs*-tuh *zah*-nyah-tuh?

Boo-*raw* uhb-*sloojh* i-vahn-i-yuh
Gulu-mlch-*nah*-yah
Yah mehn-*yah* zah-kah-*zahn* naw-mir nah...
   si-*vawd*-nyahsh-nyoo-yoo nawch
   tree dnah
   uhd-nuh-*vuh* chehl-uh-vehk-ah
   dvookh *chehl*-uh-vehk
Skawl-kuh *staw*-yit *naw*-mir nah...?
   uh-*deen* dehn
   ni-*deh*-loo
Yah by khuh-*tehl* (khuh-teh-luh, *f.*)
   puh-guh-vuh-*reet* sahd-mihn-is-strah-*tuhr*-uhm.
Klooch uht *maw*-yeh-vuh naw-mir-ah, puh-*jhahl*-stuh.
Nyeh bis-puh-*koi*-teh mehn-*yah* duh...
Yah yiz-*jhah* yoo v
   chuh-*sawv* oo-trah
Puhd-guh-*tawv*-teh, puh-*jhahl*-stuh, scheht.

Ti-li-*fawn*
Gdeh ti-li-*fawn* uhv-tuh-maht?
Puhz-vuh-*neet*, puh-*jhahl*-stuh, zah mehn-*yah?*
Puhsh-li-teh, puh-*jhahl*-stuh, zah mehn-*yah*
   ti-li-*grahm*-muh?

ENGLISH	RUSSIAN

COMMUNICATIONS
(Continued)

I want to make a long distance call.	Мне нужно сделать междугородний звонок.
This is...speaking.	Это говорит...
My number is...	Мой номер...
The line is busy.	Занято.
Hold on.	Подождите у телефона.
The operator will call you.	Телефонистка вам позвонит.
There is a phone call for you.	Вас к телефону.

Postal services

Post office	Почта
Letter	Письмо
Postcard	Открытка
Stamp	Марка
Envelope	Конверт
I would like to send this...	Я хотел бы отправить это...
airmail	авиапочтой
parcel post	посылкой
registered	заказным письмом
money order	почтовым переводом
insured	застрахованным письмом
to the U.S.	в США
Which window should I go to?	В какое окошко мне обратиться?
How much is the postage?	Сколько стоит отправить это?
Please give me a receipt	Дайте мне, пожалуйста, квитанцию.

BANKS AND MONEY

What is the exchange rate on the...?	Каков обменный курс...?
dollar	доллара
ruble	рубля
franc	франка
mark	марки
I want to exchange . . . for . . .	Я хочу поменять...на...
I want to cash...	Я хочу получить деньги по...
this check	этому чеку
this traveler's check	этому дорожному чеку
I have...	У меня есть...
a bank draft	банковский вексель
a letter of credit	аккредитив
Please give me...	Пожалуйста, дайте мне...
large bills	крупные купюры
small bills	мелкие купюры
change	мелочь

RESTAURANT AND BAR

I would like...	Я выпил бы...
beer	пива
cognac	коньяка
champagne	шампанского
whiskey (and soda)	виски (с содовой)
white wine	белого вина
red wine	красного вина
vodka	водки
To your health!	За ваше здоровье!

ENGLISH PHONETIC TRANSCRIPTION

Mehn-*yeh noojh*-nuh sdehl-*aht*
  mehjh-doog-uh-*rwd*-ny.
Eh-tuh guh-vuh-*reet*...
Moi *naw*-mir...
Zuh-nyah-*taw*.
Puh-duhjh-*di*-teh oo ti-li-*fawn*-ah.
Ti-li *fawn* ist kah vahm puz-*vawn*-it.
Vuhs kti-li-*faw*-noo.

Pawch-tuh
Pis-*maw*
Uht-*kryt*-kuh
Mahr-kuh
Kuhn-*vehrt*
Yah khuh-*tehl* by uht-*prahv*-it *eh*-tuh...
  uh-veh-uh-pawch-*toi*
  puh-*syl*-koi
  zuh-kuhz-*nihm* pis-*mawm*
  pawch-tuh-vihm pi-ri-*vawd*-uhm
  zuh-struh-*khaw*-vuhn-nihm pis-*mawm*
  vuh-*meh*-ri-koo (es-sh-ah)
Vkuhk-uh-yeh awkh-*uhsh*-kaw mehn-*yeh* uh-brah-*tit*-syah?
Skawl-kuh staw-yit uht-*prahv*-it *eh*-tuh?
Dah-it-eh mehn-*yeh* puh-*jhahl*-stuh, kvi-*tahn*-tsi-yoo.

Kuh-*koi*, uhb-*mehn*-ny koors...?

  dawl-lu-ruh
  roob-*lyah*
  frahn-kuh
  mahr-*ki*
Yah khuh-*choo* puh-mi-*naht*...nah...
Yah khuh-*choo* puh-loo-*cheet dehn*-gee puh
  ch tuh-moo cheh-koo
  eh-tuh-moo duhr-*awjh*-nuh-moo *cheh*-koo
Oo mehn-*yah* yest...
  bahn-*kawv*-skee vehk-sehl
  uhk-kreh-di-*teev*
Puh-*jhahl*-stuh, *deye*-teh mehn-*yeh*...
  kroop-ny koop-*yoor*
  myel-ki koop-*yoor*
  meh-luhch

Yah khuh-*tchl*...
  pee-vuh
  kawn-yahk-ah
  shuhm-*puhn*-skuh-vuh
  vees-kee (s *saw*-duh-voi)
  beh-luh-vuh *vee*-nuh
  krahs-nuh-vuh *vee*-nuh
  vuhd-kee
Zuh *vah*-sheh zduh-*raw*-veh!

ENGLISH	**RUSSIAN**

RESTAURANTS
(Continued)

Let's have another round!	Давайте повторим!
Please bring us...	Пожалуйста, принесите нам...
the menu	меню
the wine list	прейскурант вин
a knife	нож
a fork	вилку
a spoon	ложку
a napkin	салфетку
Please take our order...	Примите, пожалуйста, заказ...
(for) appetizers	(на) закуски
(for) the first course	(на) первое
(for) the second course	(на) второе
(for) dessert	(на) дессерт
Beef	Говядина
Ham	Ветчина
Chicken	Куры
Fish	Рыба
Soup	Суп
Salad	Салат
Bread	Хлеб
I did not order this.	Я этого не заказывал.
Take it away.	Унесите это.
The check, please.	Счет, пожалуйста.
Pay the cashier.	Заплатите в кассу.
Keep the change.	Сдачи не надо.

ENTERTAINMENT

What are the places of interest here?	Что здесь есть интересного?
Museum	Музей
Gallery	Галерея
Monument	Памятник
Garden	Парк
Cinema	Кино
Concert	Концерт
Ballet	Балет
Opera	Опера
Theater	Театр
What (film, play, ballet, concert, opera) is playing tonight?	Какой (фильм, спектакль, балет, концерт, опера) идет сегодня?
Are there any seats available?	Есть ли билеты?
How much are the seats in the...	Сколько стоят билеты...
orchestra	в партер?
balcony	на балкон?
What time does the performance start?	Когда начало?
What time is it over?	Когда кончается?

SHOPPING

I would like to go shopping today.	Я бы хотел пойти сегодня за покупками.
I would like to go to a...	Я хотел бы пойти...
grocery	в продовольственный магазин
farmers market	на рынок
pharmacy	в аптеку

ENGLISH PHONETIC TRANSCRIPTION

Duh-*vah*-yit-eh puhv-*tawr*-ihm!
Puh-*jhahl*-stuh, pri-ni-*seet*-eh nahm...
  mi-*noo*
  preh-*yuhs*-koor-ahnt veen
  nawsh
  veel-koo
  lawsh-koo
  suhl-*feht*-koo
Pri-*mit*-eh, puh-*jhahl*-stuh, zuh-*kuhz*...
  (nuh) zuh-*koos*-kee
  (nuh) *pyer*-vuh-yeh
  (nuh) ftuh-*ruh*-yeh
  (nuh) deh-*sehrt*
Guhv-*ya*-dee-nah
Vit-chi-*nuh*
Koor-ih
Rih-bah
Soop
Suh-*laht*
Khlehb
Yah *eh*-tuh-vuh nyeh zuh-*kah*-zy-vuhl.
On neh-*sih*-teh et-tuh
Scheht, puh-*jhahl*-stuh.
Zuh-pluh-*tee*-teh vkahs-soo.
Sdah-chee nyeh *nah*-duh.

Shtaw zdehs yest ihn-tehr-*ehs*-nuh-vuh?

  Moo-*zey*
  Guhl-li-*reh*-yuh
  Pah-myaht-nik
  Pahrk
  Ki-*nuh*
  Kuhn-*tsehrt*
  Buhl-*yeht*
  Aw-pi-ruh
  Ti-*ahtr*
Kuh-*koi* (feelm, *spehk*-tuh-kuhl, buhl-*yeht*, kuhn-*tsehrt*,
  aw-pir-ny) ee-*deht* si-*vawd*-nyah?
Yehst li bihl-*yeh*-tee?
Skawl-kuh *stoi*-yaht bihl-*yeh*-tee...?
  vpahr-tehr
  nah buhl-*kuwn*
Kuhg-*dah* nuh-*chah*-luh?

Kuhg-*dah* kuhn-*chah*-yit-suh?

Yah by khuh-*tehl* poi-*tee* si-*vawd*-nyah zuh
  puh-*koop*-kuh-mee.
Yah khuh-*tehl* by poi-*tee*...
  vpruh-duh-*vuhl*-stvehn-ny mahg-ah-*zeen*
  nah *ryn*-uhk
  vuhp-*teh*-koo

ENGLISH	RUSSIAN

SHOPPING
(Continued)

bookshop	в книжный магазин
candy shop	в кондитерский магазин
bakery	в булочную
department store	в универмаг
How much does it cost?	Сколько это стоит?
It is too expensive.	Это слишком дорого.
Do you have anything...?	Есть ли у вас что-нибудь...
cheaper	подешевле?
better	получше?
more expensive	подороже?
I (don't) like it.	Мне это (не) нравится.
May I try it on?	Можно примерить?
That is all.	Больше ничего.
Where can I pay?	Где можно заплатить?

EMERGENCIES

Help!	Помогите!
Fire!	Пожар!
Police!	Милиция!
Stop!	Стой!
Go away!	Уходи!
Get a...	Позовите...
doctor	врача
policeman	милиционера
I (*m*)/he am/is injured.	Я (он) ранен
I (*f*)/she am/is injured.	Я (она) ранена
I have a pain here.	Здесь болит.
Notify...	Известите...
my husband	моего мужа
my wife	мою жену
my friend	моего друга
the American Embassy	Американское посольство

GLOSSARY OF BUSINESS TERMINOLOGY

accountant, bookkeeper	бухгалтер
advertisement	реклама
advice	совет
advisor	советник
agreement	соглашение
bank	банк
bankruptcy	банкротство
black market	черный рынок
board of directors	совет директоров
chief	босс, начальник
business (adj.), business-like	деловой
businessman	бизнесмен
capitalist	капиталист
cent	цент
cheap	дешевый
client	клиент
clientele	клиентура
commercial	коммерческий

ENGLISH PHONETIC TRANSCRIPTION

vkneejh-ny muh-guh-*zeen*
vkahn-*deet*-ir-skee mahg-ah-*zeen*
vbool-ahch-ny-yoo
voo-ni-vir-*mahg*
Skawl-kuh *eh*-tuh *staw*-yit?
Eh-tuh *sleesh*-kuhm *duh*-ruh-guh.
Yehst-li oo vahs shtaw-nih-bood . . .
   puh-di-*shehv*-leh
   puh-*looch*-sheh
   puh-duh-*raw*-zheh
Mehn-*yeh eh*-tuh (nyeh) *nrah*-vi-tsuh.
Mawjh-nuh prih-*mir*-it?
Buhl-sheh *neech*-ee-vuh.
Gdyeh *muhjh*-nuh zah-plah-*teet*?

Paw-muhg-*eet*-eh
Puh-*zhahr!*
Mil-*lee*-tsi-yuh!
Stoi!
Oo-*khuh*-dee!
Puh-zuh-*vee*-teh...
   vrah-chah
   mih-*lee*-tsi-uhn-ehr-ah
Yah/awn *ruh*-nin.
Yah/*aw*-nuh *ruh*-ni-nuh.
Zdehs buhl-*it*
Iz-vy-*steet*-eh...
   muh-yeh-*vo moo*-jhuh
   muh-*yoo* jhy-*noo*
   muh-yeh-*vo, droo*-guh
   Uh-mi-ri-*kahn*-skuh-yeh puh-*suhl*-stvah

bookh-*gahl*-tyer
reh-*kla*-mah
sohv-*yet*
sohv-*yet*-neek
sah-glah-*she*-nee-yeh

bahnk
bonk *rote*-svoh
chyore-nee *ry*-nuhk
sohv-*yet* dir-ek-*tuhr*-uhv
nah-*chahl*-neek
dyell-loh-*voy*
bihz-nehz-mehn

kah-pee-tah-*leest*
tsehnt
di-*shaw*-vy
klee-yent
klee-yen-*too*-rah
komm-*myehr*-chess-kee

ENGLISH	RUSSIAN
company, business, enterprise	компания, бизнес, предприятие
contract	контракт
corporation	корпорация
cost	стоимость
credit	кредит
credit card	кредитная карточка
customer	заказчик
deficit	дефицит
dollars	доллары
earnings	доходы
economy	экономика
employee	работник
employer	работодатель
employment, work	работа
equipment	оборудование
expensive	дорогой
export	экспорт
finance	финансы
financial	финансовый
firm	фирма
foreign (hard) currency	твердая валюта
foreign trade	внешняя торговля
free market	свободный рынок
goods	товары
import	импорт
income	доход
industry	промышленность
inflation	инфляция
investor	вкладчик
joint venture	совместное предприятие
loan	заем
management (of something)	управление
market price	рыночная цена
meeting	деловая встреча
negotiate	вести переговоры
office (study)	кабинет
owner	владелец
payment, charge, fee	плата
price	цена
private property	частная собственность
production	производство
products	продукты
profit	прибыль
sale (of property)	продажа
stock exchange	биржа
tariff	тариф
tax	налог
trade	торговля
wages, pay, salary	заработная плата

ENGLISH PHONETIC TRANSCRIPTION

pred-pree-*yaht*-ee-yeh
kohn-trahkt
korpa-*rahts*-ee-yah
staw-ee-muhst
kre-*deet*
kre-*deet*-nai-yah *car*-toch-kah
zah-*kahz*-chihk

dyeff-ee-*tseet*
dawl-luh-ry
duh-*khaw*-dih
eh-kuh *nawm* ih kah
rah-*boat*-neek
rah-boat-a-*daht*-yell
ruh-*baw*-tuh
ah-bah-*rood*-o-vahn-ee-yeh
duh-ruh-goi
echs-port

fee-*nahn*-see
fee-*nahn*-so-vwee
feerm-ah
voh-*lute*-ah
vnyesh-nai-ya tore-*gohv*-lyah
svuh-*bawd*-ny *rih*-nuk
toh-*vahr*-ee

eem-port
doh-*khode*
pro-*mish*-lyen-nost
een-*flyah*-tsee-yah
vklaad-cheek
sohv-*myest*-noi-yeh pred-pree-*yaht*-ee-yeh
zah-*yome*
oo-prahv-*lyen*-ee-yeh
rih-nohch-nai-yah tsi-*nah*
vstretch-ah
piehr-reh-gah-*vore*-ee
ka-been-*nyet*
vlah-*dyell*-yets

plata
tsyena
chahs-nai-yah *sobe*-tsvyen-nost
proh-eez-*vohd*-stvah
proh-*dook*-tee
pree-bwihl

pro-*daj*-ah
beer-jah

tah-*reef*
nah-*lohg*
tore-*gohv*-lyah
zahr-*plaht* a

Conversion Tables

LENGTH

cm	m	km	inch	foot	yard	mile
1	0.01	-	0.3937	0.0328	0.0109	-
100	1	0.001	39.37	3.2808	1.0936	0.0006
100,000	1,000	1	39,370	3280.8	1093.6	0.6214
2.5399	0.0254	-	1	0.0833	0.0277	-
30.479	0.3048	-	12	1	0.333	-
91.4400	0.9144	-	36	3	1	0.000568
-	1609.3	1.6093	-	5,280	1760	1

VOLUME

m³	cubic inch	cubic foot	cubic yard	liter	gallon (U.K.)	gallon (U.S.A.)
1	61.022	35.314	1.308	1.000	219.969	264.1
-	1	0.00058	-	-	0.0036	0.0043
0.0283	1728	1	0.037037	28.31	6.229	7.481
0.7646	46.656	27	1	764.6	168.17	201.96
0.001	61.022	0.0353	0.0013	1	0.021996	0.26417
0.0045461	277.42	0.16054	0.0059	4.546	1	1.2
0.00378	231	0.13368	0.00494	3.7854	0.8326	1

AREA

m²	hectare	km²	square inch	square foot	square yard	acre
1	0.0001	.000001	1549.96	10.7637	1.1959	0.0002471
10,000	1	0.01	-	107,637	11.959	2.471
1,000,000	100	1	-	-	-	247.104
0.0006	-	-	1	0.0069	0.0008	-
0.092903	-	-	144	1	0.111	-
0.8361	0.0083	-	1296	9	1	0.00022
4046.9	0.4047	0.004	-	43,560	4840	1

WEIGHT

gm	kg	ounce	pound
1	0.001	0.035	0.002
1000	1	35.274	2.205
28.35	0.028	1	0.063
453.59	0.454	16	1

$$°F = \frac{9}{5}°C + 32°$$

$$°C = \frac{5}{9}(°F - 32°)$$

NOTE: Dashes denote quantities too large or small to be of practical value.

CELSIUS & FAHRENHEIT

°C	°F
100	212
90	194
80	176
70	158
60	140
50	122
40	104
30	86
20	68
10	50
0	32

°F	°C
100	37.7
90	32.2
80	26.7
70	21.1
60	15.6
50	10.0
40	4.4
30	-1.1
20	-6.7
10	-12.2
0	-17.7

APPENDIX

SOVIET REPUBLICS AND THEIR CAPITALS

Republic	Capital	Republic	Capital
Armenia	Yerevan	**Lithuania**	Vilnius
Azerbaidzhan	Baku	**Moldavia**	Kishinev
Byelorussia	Minsk	**Russia**	Moscow
Estonia	Tallinn	**Tadzhikistan**	Dushanbe
Georgia	Tbilisi	**Turkmenia**	Ashkhabad
Kazakhstan	Alma-Ata	**Ukraine**	Kiev
Kirghizia	Frunze	**Uzbekistan**	Tashkent
Latvia	Riga		

CHRONOLOGY OF RUSSIAN / SOVIET HISTORY

Beginning of Russian History (862 AD). A Scandinavian leader, Rurik, and his followers take control of the Western Russian heartland, establishing the first Slavic state, with its capital at Kiev.

Byzantium (989). Christianity comes to Kievan Russia from Constantinople, bringing with it the cultural dominance of Byzantium. The year 1989 is the Millennium, marking a thousand years of Christianity.

Chronicles (early 12th century). First recorded history from Russia.

Mongol Conquest (1240–1480). The Golden Horde of Genghis Khan and his successors overruns the Eurasian corridor from China to Poland, submerging Kievan Russia, dispersing its people, and subjecting them to more than two centuries of Mongol rule, which cuts Russia off from the West and imposes the imprint of harsh Oriental despotism.

Rise of Muscovy (1263–1682). Dukes of Muscovy, acting first as agents and tax collectors of the Mongols, gradually expand power and territory, take the lead in throwing off Mongol domination, and establish their rule in the Russian heartland.

Imperial Period: Peter I to Catherine II (1682–1796). Territorial expansion of Russia to a great transcontinental empire, from central Europe to the Pacific.

Napoleonic Wars (1796–1814). Russian involvement in the French Revolutionary and Napoleonic wars, climaxed by Napoleon's invasion of 1812, the burning of Moscow, Napoleon's retreat, and the triumphant entry of the Russian army into Paris.

Autocracy and Reform (1815–1914). Alternating and competing trends of Czarist autocracy and political reform, highlighted by the freeing of the serfs in 1861.

War and Revolution (1904–1917). An abortive revolution in 1905, sparked by political dissatisfaction and military defeat by Japan. Severe losses at Germany's hands in World War I lead to collapse of the monarchy and eventual Bolshevik seizure of power.

Civil War, Communism and the New Economic Policy (1917–1928). Bolshevik rule challenged by bloody civil war and foreign (including U.S.) military intervention. The Kronstadt revolt of Soviet sailors in 1921 leads Lenin to adopt a more moderate economic recovery program, the New Economic Policy, a compromise between a centrally controlled and a decentralized economy. This is the period to which Gorbachev now links his "radical reform," although his use of Lenin's views and policies is quite selective.

Stalinism (1928–1953). Stalin wins the succession struggle after Lenin's death and launches a program of rapid industrialization. This program emphasized heavy and defense industries and forced collectivization of agriculture, accompanied by pervasive purges of the party and terrorization of the society as a whole. The five-year plans industrialize the U.S.S.R., but the Stalinist terror claims some 20 million Soviet lives.

World War II (1941–1945). The uneasy alliance between Hitler and Stalin, during which they divide Poland and annex the Baltic states, is ended in June 1941 with the German invasion. Eventual victory over Nazi Germany is achieved only after most of European Russia is occupied and laid waste. There are 20 million Soviet casualties (in addition to significant indirect civilian losses).

Stalin's Successors (1953–1985). Khrushchev wins the succession struggle after Stalin's death (1953), launches a de-Stalinization campaign, and dominates Soviet politics until his ouster in 1964. Brezhnev gradually emerges as the dominant figure in the new regime, marked by cautious domestic policies, steady build-up of military power and the central bureaucracy, and economic slowdown and eventual stagnation. After Brezhnev's death in November 1982, Yuri Andropov, former KGB chief, emerges as the new party leader, initiates anti-corruption campaign and some economic reforms, but is hampered by chronic illness and dies in February 1984 after only 15 months in power. Andropov is succeeded by Konstantin Chernenko, a long-time party bureaucrat and protégé of Brezhnev. Chronically ill and 73 years old at the time of his accession, Chernenko dies 13 months later and is succeeded by Mikhail Gorbachev on March 11, 1985.

Gorbachev and *Perestroika* (1985–present). With Gorbachev's succession, the transition of leadership following Brezhnev's death appears to be concluded. In his first four years, Gorbachev institutes considerable personnel changes in leading party and government bodies and begins to develop far-reaching changes in economic, political, social, and foreign policy under the catchword *perestroika,* or restructuring and reform. How successful *perestroika* will be in reversing the stagnation of the Brezhnev years remains to be seen.

SOVIET LAWS CONCERNING JOINT VENTURES, FOREIGN ENTERPRISES AND FOREIGN NATIONALS

§ Decree of the Presidium of the Supreme Soviet, No. 6362-XI, January 13, 1987, "On Questions Concerning the Establishment in the Territory of the U.S.S.R. and Operation of Joint Ventures, International Amalgamations and Organizations with the Participation of Soviet and Foreign Organizations, Firms and Management Bodies."

§ Decree of the U.S.S.R. Council of Ministers, No. 49, January 13, 1987, "On the Establishment in the Territory of the U.S.S.R. and Operation of Joint Ventures with the Participation of Soviet Organizations and Firms From Capitalist and Developing Countries."

§ Decree of the U.S.S.R. Council of Ministers, No. 1074, September 17, 1987, "On Additional Measures to Streamline Foreign Economic Activity in the New Conditions of Economic Management."

§ Decree of the U.S.S.R. Ministry of Finance, No. 224, November 24, 1987, "Regulations Concerning the Procedures for Registering Joint Ventures, International Amalgamations and Organizations Established in the Territory of the U.S.S.R. with the Participation of Soviet and Foreign Organizations, Firms and Authorities."

§ U.S.S.R. State Committee for Prices, U.S.S.R. State Planning Committee, U.S.S.R. Ministry of Finance, U.S.S.R. Ministry of Foreign Trade, and U.S.S.R. State Committee for Foreign Economic Relations, "Procedures for Assessing the Land, Natural Resources, Building and Structures Forming Part of the Soviet Partners' Contribution to the Authorized Capital of Joint Ventures, or Leased to Joint Ventures for Temporary Use."

§ Decree of the State Committee for Supplies, No. 74, June 4, 1987, "Supplies of Materials and Equipment to Joint Ventures Established in the U.S.S.R. Territory with the Participation of Other Countries and Foreign Firms and Marketing of Their Products."

§ Instruction of the Ministry of Finance, No. 45-15-1, June 5, 1987, "On the Procedure Governing the Insurance of the Assets and Interests of Joint Ventures."

§ Letter of the U.S.S.R. Ministry of Finance and Central Board of Statistics, No. 53/13-09, February 27, 1987, "Accounting and Bookkeeping at Joint Ventures, International Amalgamations and Organizations Established in the Territory of the U.S.S.R."

§ Instruction of the Ministry of Finance, No. 124, May 4, 1987, "On Taxation of Joint Ventures."

§ Decree of the U.S.S.R. Ministry of Finance No. 226, November 30, 1987, "On Partial Amendment of the Taxation of Joint Ventures."

§ Decree of the State Bank of the U.S.S.R., No. 1015, and Bank of Foreign Trade of the U.S.S.R., No. 149, September 22, 1987, "Procedure for Crediting and Settlement of Accounts of Joint Ventures, International Amalgamations and Organizations of the U.S.S.R. and other CMEA Member-Countries, as well as of Joint Ventures with the Participation of Soviet Organizations and Firms from Capitalist and Developing Countries."

§ Law of the U.S.S.R. on the Legal Status of Foreign Nationals in the U.S.S.R. Adopted June 24, 1981, Gazette of the U.S.S.R. Supreme Soviet, November 26, 1981; item 836.

CHECKLIST FOR A JOINT VENTURE AGREEMENT

☐ *Introduction*
☐ Definitions
☐ Formation, Name, Location, Principal Place of Business
  and Term of Joint Venture
  • Partners' Interest in the Joint Venture
☐ Purpose, Objectives and Mutual Understandings
☐ Total Amount of Investment and Ownership Capital
  • Contributions to Capital   • Timing of Capital Contributions
☐ Creation of Statutory Fund
  • Partners' Interest in   • Additional Contributions
    Statutory Fund   • Alterations in
  • Initial Capital Contributions   Partnership Interests
☐ Profits and Losses
  • Accounting and Fiscal Year
  • Payment of Start-up Costs (U.S. Party)
☐ Annual Distribution of Profits and Withdrawal of Capital
  • Undistributed Profits   • Payments to Partners for
  • Amount and Method of Distribution   Rendering of Services
    and Withdrawals   or Provision of Goods
☐ Administration and Fiscal Matters
  • Books and Records   • Release of Information
  • Bank Accounts
☐ Responsibilities (Soviet Party)
  • Services
  • Licenses and Registration   • U.S.S.R. Equipment
  • Investment Incentives   • Financing
  • Utilities   • Prices and Profit Margin
  • Representatives (U.S. Party)   • Cooperation (U.S. Party)
☐ Responsibilities (U.S. Party)
  • Services   • Cooperation (Soviet Party)
  • Financing
☐ Supply and Purchase of Equipment and Services
  • Equipment
  • Commitments and Obligations   • Insurance Against
    of the Partners   Third Party Claims
  • Liability for Breach of Contract   • Cooperation and Assistance
☐ Annual Business Plans
  • Approval of Business Plans
☐ Trademark and Trade Names
☐ Standard Operating Procedures
☐ Loans to the Joint Venture
☐ Assignment of Joint Venture Interest
  • Priority Right of First Refusal of Partners
☐ Settlement of Disputes
  • Consultations   • Arbitration
☐ Termination of Joint Venture
  • Transfer of U.S. Party Partnership • Renegotiation of Terms
  • U.S. Party Partnership Interest   of Agreement
☐ *Force Majeure*
  • *Force Majeure* Defined   • Cessation of *Force Majeure*
  • Effect of *Force Majeure*   • Termination of Agreement
  • Notice of *Force Majeure*   Upon *Force Majeure*
☐ Representation and Warranties for Both Parties
☐ General Provisions
  • Notices   • Entire Agreement; Amendments
  • Applicable Law   • No Waiver of Rights
  • Economic Adjustment   • Charter
  • Tax and Investment Incentives   • Language
  • Severability   • Headings
  • Confidentiality

SOVIET TRADE EXHIBITIONS, 1990–1991

Note: Additional information on Trade Exhibitions in the Soviet Union
can be obtained from: Expocentr U.S.S.R. CCI, 1a Sokolnichcsky Val,
Moscow 107113, U.S.S.R. Telex: 411185 EXPO SU.

1990

May 22–31 Moscow	Public Health, Medical Equipment and Pharmaceuticals
May 23–30 Yerevan	Machinery and Instruments for Mining and Processing of Stone Materials
May 24–31 Cherkassy	Sugar Beet Cultivation, Processing Machinery and Equipment
June 1–30 Minsk	Technological Devices for Construction Sites
June 6–13 Ashkhabad	Solar Energy Engineering
July 12–19 Donetsk	Mechanization and Automation for Refractory Products Manufacture
Aug. 6–15 Leningrad	Modern Means for Reproduction and Utilization of Biological Water Resources
Aug. 26–Sept. 9 Donetsk	Coal Industry: Equipment, Machinery, Instruments and Automation Means
Sept. 9–13 Moscow	Agricultural Machinery, Equipment and Instruments
Sept. 9–20 Riga	Energy Conservation for Agricultural Installations, Construction and Production
Oct. 4–11 Kiev	Chinaware and Earthenware Manufacturing Equipment
Oct. 18–25 Moscow	Computers and Scientific Information Products
Oct. 18–25 Alma-Ata	Automation Technology for Light Industry
Oct. 19–26 Moscow	Equipment and Instruments for Geology, Geophysics and Cartography
Nov. 22–29 Moscow	Equipment for Production of Electronic Components

1991

Jan. 17–24 Moscow	Consumer Goods — CONSUMEXPO '91
Feb. Moscow	Equipment for Production of Rehabilitation Devices
Feb. Moscow	Technology for Law Enforcement
Mar. 20–27 Moscow	Equipment for Hotels — TOURINDUSTRIA
Mar. 20–27 Kiev	Equipment, Technologies, New Types and Forms of Public Amenity Services — SLUZHBA BYTA '91
Mar. 21–28 Moscow	Equipment for Production of Clocks and Watches — INCHASMASH '91

Mar. 21–28 Moscow	Equipment for Production of Automobile Tires — SHINA '91
April 11–18 Moscow	Equipment for Diagnostics and Repair of Automotive Vehicles — AVTOSERVIS '91
April 12–19 Tashkent	Scientific and Research Apparatus for Public Health — MEDAPPARATURA '91
May 20–30 Leningrad	Equipment for Welding — SVARKA '91
May 22–31 Moscow	STROYINDUSTRIA '91
May 28–June 3 Moscow	PATHOPHYSIOLOGY '91
June 6–13 Kiev	Machinery and Technology for Production of Leather Materials, Shoes, Leather Haberdashery and Accessories — KOZHPROM '91
June 13–20 Ufa	Electrophysical and Electrochemical Methodologies
June 26–July 3 Nakhodka	Instruments and Equipment for Ocean Research and Exploitation and for Production of Biologically Active Substances and Medical Preparations — BIORESOURSY OKEANA '91
June 27–July 7 Moscow	Production and Use of Aluminum and Aluminum Prefabricates — ALUMINUM '91
June 23–28 Moscow	NEURO-SURGERY '91
July 27–Aug. 2 Moscow	International Trade Fair for Trading of Equipment and Material Resources— INTEROPTTORG
Aug. 18–24 Moscow	Libraries and Culture: Their Relationship
Sept. 4–12 Moscow	Trade and Catering Equipment — INTORGMASH '91
Sept. 5–12 Kishinev	Equipment for Production of Sewn Garments, Textiles, and Tricot Products — SHVEYMASH '91
Sept. 12–19 Donetsk	Environmental Protection and Conservation — ECOLOGY '91
Sept. 12–19 Minsk	Spectroscopic Equipment for Scientific Purposes — SPECTRUM '91
Sept. 17–23 Novosibirsk	Equipment, Technology, and Control Means in Production of Catalysts — KATALIZ '91
Oct. 17–24 Minsk	Equipment and Technology for Furniture and Woodworking Industries — DEREVUBRABOTKA '91
Oct. 17–24 Riga	Technical Means and Technology for Urban Economic Development in a Modern Town — KOMMUNALNAYA TEKHNIKA '91

Nov. 20–27 Baku	Electric Household Appliances — BYTPRIBOR '91
Nov. 26–Dec. 4 Moscow	Communication Equipment — SVIAZ '91
Dec. 5–12 Yerevan	Equipment and Technology for Processing Raw Materials Using Recycled Polymers — VTORPOLYMERMASH '91
(date not fixed) Tbilisi	Modern Solutions for Dwelling, Civil, Rural, and Transport Construction
(date not fixed) Tbilisi	Local Networks Based on PC's and Computerized Systems and CAD/CAM Systems

ACCREDITED U.S. COMPANIES IN THE U.S.S.R.

Location of U.S. Personnel and Telephone Numbers

FIRM	REPRESENTATIVE IN MOSCOW
Abbott Laboratories Abbott Park 14th and Sheridan Road North Chicago, IL 60064 Tel.: (312) 937-6100	Richard McMahon Head of Representation Gruzinsky Per. 3, Apt. 162 Tel.: 254-1774, 254-6852 Telex: 413340 ABLAB SU
Allis Chalmers P.O. Box 512 Milwaukee, WI 53214 Tel.: (414) 475-2000	Kurt Ohlsoon (Sala, Sweden) Head of Representation Krasnopresnenskaya Nab. 12 World Trade Center, Room 901 Tel.: 253-2970, 253-2971, 253-2972 Telex: 413419 ACMOS SU
American Express Company American Express Plaza New York, NY 10004 Tel.: (212) 480-2000	William C. Fisher Vice President 21-A Sadovo Kudrinskaya Tel.: 254-2111, 254-4305, 254-4495, 254-4505 Telex: 413075 AMEXM SU
Armco International, Inc. 703 Curtis Street Middletown, OH 45043 Tel.: (513) 425-6541	W. O'Hara, N.Y. Head of Representation U1 Smolenskaya, 8 Hotel Belgrade-2, Room 821 Tel.: 248-1865 Telex: 413496 ARMCO SU
Baker & McKenzie 815 Connecticut Avenue, N.W. Washington, DC 20006 Tel.: (202) 452-7000	Paul J. Melling Arthur L. George John P. Hewko Pushkin Plaza Bolshoi Gnezdnykovsky Per. 7 Tel.: 200-4906, 200-6167, 200-6186 Telex: 413671 BAKER SU
Bank of America Bank of America Center P.O. Box 37000 San Francisco, CA 94137 Tel.:(415) 622-3456	Hartmut Heimann Krasnopresnenskaya Nab. 12 World Trade Center, Room 1605 Tel.: 253-7054, 253-1910, 253-1911 Telex: 413189 BOFA SU

FIRM	REPRESENTATIVE IN MOSCOW
Caterpillar Overseas S.A. 100 N.E. Adams Street Peoria, IL 61629 Tel.: (309) 675-1000	Felix Calonder Director of U.S.S.R. Representation Pokrovsky Bulvd. 4/17 Apt. 13, Floor 6 Tel.: 207-5658, 207-1007, 207-2625 Telex: 413202 CAT SU
Chase Manhattan Bank One Chase Manhattan Plaza New York, NY 10015 Tel.: (212) 552-2222 (Int'l line)	John P. Minneman Vice President & Representative (Moscow and New York) Krasnopresnenskaya Nab. 12 World Trade Center, Room 1709 Tel.: 253-8377, 253-2865, 230-2174 Telex: 413912 CHASE SU
Chilewich Corporation 120 Wall Street New York, NY 10005 Tel.: (212) 344-3400	Richard Aelion-Moss Head of Representation Kursovoi Per. 9, Apt. 2 Tel.: 202-1904, 202-1740, 230-2091 (Int'l line) Telex: 413211 CHILW SU
Control Data 8100 34th Avenue, South Minneapolis, MN 55440 Tel.: (612) 853-8100	Helmut Koller Head of Representation (Vienna) Krasnopresnenskaya Nab. 12 World Trade Center, Room 2006 Tel.: 253-8379 Telex: 413311 CDC SU
Cooper Industries, Inc. First City Tower Building Suite 4000 Houston, TX 77002 Tel.: (713) 654-4451	Richard Ciochetti Manager Per. Sadovskikh 5 Floor 5, Apt. 12 Tel.: 209-6520, 230-2133 Telex: 413376 CIMO SU
Corning Glass Works Houghton Park Corning, NY 14830 Tel.: (607) 974-9000	Dick O'Brien (Corning, NY) Hotel National, Room 378 Tel.: 203-4908
Dow Chemical Co. Midland, MI 48640 Tel.: (517) 636-1000	S. Kostic Director Pokrovsky Bulvd. 4/17 Apt. 9, Floor 4 Tel.: 297-0074, 297-0075, 297-0077, 297-0078 Telex: 413217 DOW SU
Dresser Industries, Inc. 1505 Elm Street Dallas, TX 75221 Tel.: (214) 740-6000	Bob N. Cook Director 1 Ulitsa Lunacharskovo 7, Floor 6, Apt. 16/17 Tel.: 203-0055 Telex: 413166 DRESR SU

Construction &
  Mining Equipment
  Division of Dresser Industries
1505 Elm Street
Dallas, TX 75221
Tel.: (214) 740-6000
	Ivan L. (Ike) Jones
	Resident Director
	1 Ulitsa Lunacharskovo 7,
	Floor 6, Apt. 16/17,
	Tel.: 203-7924, 202-1094, 202-1229
	Telex: 413337 CME SU

FIRM	REPRESENTATIVE IN MOSCOW
E. I. Dupont de Nemours 1008 Market Street Wilmington, DE 19898 Tel.: (302) 774-2421	Paul T. Cavanaugh Director Pokrovsky Bulvd. 4/17 Apt. 26, Floor 6 Tel.: 207-6503, 207-6514, 207-5714, 230-2215
E.I. Dupont de Nemours, Agrochemical Dept. 1008 Market Street Wilmington, DE 19898 Tel.: (302) 774-2421	D.J. Meadows Krasnopresnenskaya Nab. Office 1503 A, 15th Floor Tel.: 253-2498, 253-2861, 253-9073, 253-9074 Telex: 413555 DUMOS SU
FMC Corporation 209 E. Randolph Drive Chicago, IL 60601 Tel.: (312) 861-6000	Bill Worner Head of Representation Gruzinsky Per. 3, Apt. 197 Tel.: 254-4119, 254-7719 Telex: 413979 FMC SU
General Electric Company 570 Lexington Avenue New York, NY 10022 Tel.: (212) 750-2000	Frederic Drake Vice President Head of Representation Pokrovsky Bulvd. 4/17 Apt. 20, Floor 3 Tel.: 297-2995, 230-2166, 207-5919, 230-2785 Telex: 413236 GEMOS SU
Hewlett-Packard Company 3000 Hanover Street Palo Alto, CA 94304 Tel.: (415) 857-1501	Dean Terry Head of Representation Pokrovsky Bulvd. 4/17 Apt. 12, Floor 6 Tel.: 923-5001 Telex: 413225 HPCO SU
Honeywell, Inc. 2701 4th Avenue, South Minneapolis, MN 55408 Tel.: (612) 870-5200	Paul Lomauro Director/Moscow Office Tryokhprudny Per. 11/13 Floor 3 Tel.: 299-6543 Telex: 413255 HON SU
IBM Old Orchard Road Armonk, NY 10504 Tel.: (914) 765-1900	Jim Donick Head of Representation Pokrovsky Bulvd. 4/17 Office 6, Floor 3 Tel.: 207-5597, 207-5598, 207-6244, 207-3119 Telex: 413232 IBM SU
Ingersoll-Rand Company 200 Chestnut Ridge Road Woodcliff Lake, NJ 07675 Tel.: (201) 537-0123	Italo Poletti (Milan, Italy) Krasnopresnenskaya Nab. 12 World Trade Center, Room 1101 Tel.: 253-7151, 253-2655 Telex: 413969 INGR U
Monssanto Company 800 N. Lindberg Blvd. St. Louis, MO 63166 Tel.: (314) 694-1000	François Duvalet Representative Krasnopresnenskaya Nab. 12 World Trade Center, Room 1209 Tel.: 253-1683, 253-8644, 230-2173, 253-1685 Telex: 413314 MONSA SU

FIRM	REPRESENTATIVE IN MOSCOW
Occidental Petroleum 10889 Wilshire Blvd. Los Angeles, CA 90024 Tel.: (213)897-1700	Allen Spirytus Head of Representation (New York, NY) Krasnopresnenskaya Nab. 12 World Trade Center, Room 1409 Tel.: 253-2268, 253-2269, 253-2270, 253-2266 Telex: 413168 OXYM SU
Pan American World Airways Vanderbilt Ave. and 45th St. New York, NY 10166 Tel.: (212) 880-1400	Jennifer Young, Director Krasnopresnenskaya Nab. 12 World Trade Center, Room 1102 Tel.: 253-2658, 253-2659 230-2256 Airport tel.: 578-2737, 578-2738 Telex: 413089 MOWPA SU
Philipp Brothers, Inc. A Division of Salomon, Inc. 1221 Avenue of the Americas New York, NY 10036 Tel.: (212) 575-5900	Arie de Knecht Director Pokrovsky Bulvd. 4/17 Apt. 22, Floor 4 Tel.: 207-6265, 207-8734, 208-6262, 230-2532 Telex: 413219 PBMOW SU 413103 PBMOW SU
Satra Corporation 1211 Avenue of the Americas New York, NY 10036 Tel.: (212) 354-3939	Greg Oztemel Chief Representative Tryokhprudny Per. 11/13 Floor 1 Tel.: 299-9169, 299-9529, 299-2069, 230-2177 Telex: 413129 SATRA SU
U.S.-U.S.S.R. Marine Resources (SOVAM) 4215 21st Avenue West, Room 201 Seattle, WA 98199 Tel.: (206) 285-6424	Anthony Allison National Hotel, Suite 450 Marx Prospect Tel.: 203-5466, 230-2214 Telex: 413052 SOVAM SU
U.S.-U.S.S.R. Trade and Economic Council 805 Third Avenue New York, NY 10036 Tel.: (212) 644-4550	Edward A. Perper Senior Vice President 3 Shevchenko Nab. Tel.: 243-5621, 243-5494, 243-5228, 243-5470, 243-4028 Telex: 413212 ASTEC SU

SOURCES

U.S. Department of Commerce U.S.S.R. Division Room 3413 Washington, DC 20230 Tel.: (202) 377-4655	U.S. Commercial Office, Moscow U.S. Embassy Moscow APO New York 09862 Tel.: 255-4848 Telex: 413205 USCO SU